Beginner's Guide to *Needlecrafts*

Knitting • Crochet • Cross Stitch • Patchwork • Sewing

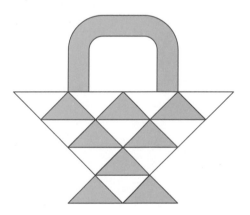

Beginner's Guide to
Needlecrafts

Knitting • Crochet • Cross Stitch • Patchwork • Sewing

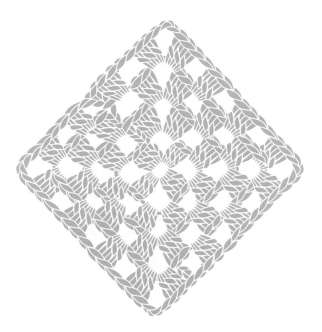

ARCTURUS

To Thelma M. Nye, craft editor at B. T. Batsford Ltd for over thirty years and friend and advisor to many grateful authors and designers

Sewing projects devised by Sara Gerlings

ARCTURUS

This edition published in 2012 by Arcturus Publishing Limited
26/27 Bickels Yard, 151–153 Bermondsey Street,
London SE1 3HA

ISBN: 978-1-84858-390-0
AD002114EN

Written by Charlotte Gerlings
Illustrated by David Woodroffe

Printed in Singapore

Back cover fabrics and threads (see numbering below):

1 *Aida (block weave) fabric*   2 *Evenweave fabric*   3 *Perle [pearl] cotton twist*   4 *6-stranded polyester*
5 *6-stranded rayon*   6 *6-stranded cotton*   7 *Blending filament*   8 *Metallic hand- or machine
embroidery thread*   9 *Metallic twist for embroidery, tassels and cords (divisible)*   10 *6-stranded
metallic polyester*   11 *Matt soft cotton (stranded)*   12 *Perle [pearl] cotton twist, plain and variegated*

Materials provided and photographed by kind permission of DMC Creative World Ltd
(visit www.dmccreative.co.uk to find out more), and Madeira UK (www.madeira.co.uk)

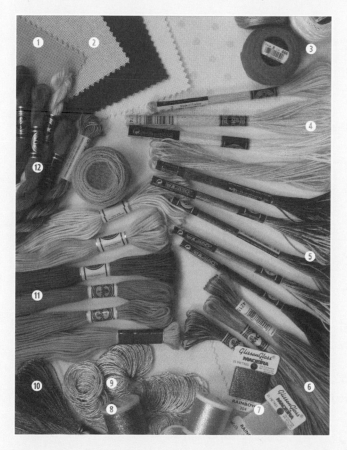

Back cover pattern samples (see numbering below):

1 *Double moss [moss] stitch*   2 *Basketweave stitch*   3 *Eyelet cable*   4 *Fishscale stitch*   5 *Chevrons*
6 *Diagonal shell pattern*   7 *Shell edging*

CONTENTS

KNITTING AND CROCHET 146

INTRODUCTION

There is something truly satisfying about making things with your own hands that begins even before the work itself. From the moment you get an idea for a project, you have all the pleasure of choosing the design and the colours and deciding on the best materials to use. And when the item is finished, you will have created something unique to yourself.

To get you started, the *Beginner's Guide to Needlecrafts* has assembled a series of mini-tutorials on the most popular and widely practised needlecrafts: Sewing, Patchwork, Cross Stitch, and Knitting and Crochet. It aims not only to provide illustrated step-by-step instructions for absolute beginners but also to fill any gaps for those who would like to refresh the skills they learned in the past.

In addition to the essential methods and techniques, each of the featured crafts presents a list of equipment. This includes the possible use of a sewing machine, and we have plenty of detailed illustrations and advice for first-time users. There is information on various materials and the quantities required, together with tips on interpreting printed patterns. Glossaries of specific terms and abbreviations accompany each craft section; and we have devised a number of simple projects to encourage you along the way.

Completing your first needlecraft project will open your eyes and, more importantly, your imagination. Be prepared to find inspiration in all kinds of places, from the shapes, colours and textures of the natural world to those of machinery and the built environment. No matter how old the craft, there is always room for experimentation and a contemporary approach, as well as following tradition.

Ambition grows with confidence in your abilities, and you may extend your efforts to making things for family and friends; creating your own patterns and styles for objects which could become the treasured heirlooms of tomorrow.

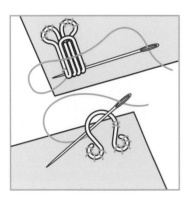

SEWING

The first needles were made from cattle bone and used to sew animal hides together with lengths of sinew. Between then and now, people have sewn clothes for warmth, tents for shelter, sails for voyages of exploration, and flags for nations. It could be argued that a needle and thread in a skilled pair of hands has played as great a part in civilization as the invention of the wheel.

However, as everyday items around the home, needles and thread are mere clutter until we unlock their potential – together with our own – and master the basic techniques of sewing. Here to help you is a step-by-step illustrated guide from threading a needle and learning basic stitches, to cutting and shaping fabric, and machine sewing with confidence. Whether you are just starting to sew or would like a refresher, this aims to be a handy reference. The terminology used is UK-standard, together with the relevant US terms in square brackets [ ] to make this a practical guide for all readers.

There are sections on all types of equipment; threads, fabrics and trimmings; how to read paper patterns; and what goes into making a garment. One complete part is devoted to the sewing machine, especially useful nowadays when more and more households are investing in one. Other sections deal with smaller but important matters such as making repairs, using a seam gauge or inserting a zip. Finally, there are three easy projects for you to practise your sewing skills, before embarking on the more ambitious ones you have planned.

PART ONE

EQUIPMENT AND MATERIALS

EQUIPMENT

A Needles, pins, pin cushion(s)

B Fabric and reels of thread

C Thimble

D Seam ripper

E Dressmaking shears

F Scissors

G Embroidery scissors

H Thread snips [nippers]

I Pinking shears

J Seam gauge

K Transparent ruler

L Fibreglass tape measure

M Tailor's chalk

N Beeswax

O Iron

P Sleeveboard for dressmaking

Q Sleeve roll and tailor's ham for dressmaking

R Sewing machine

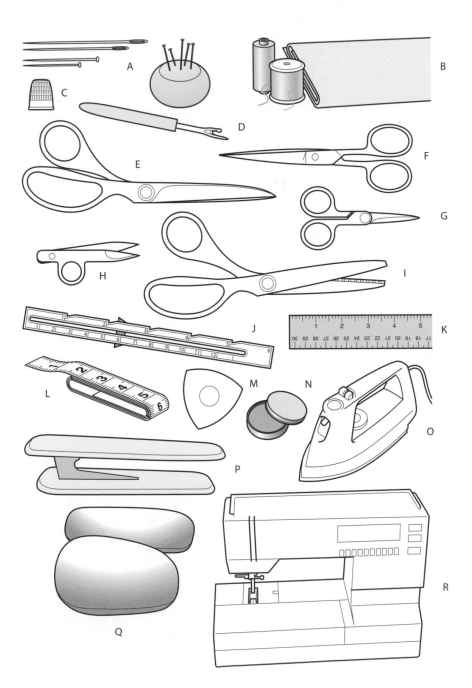

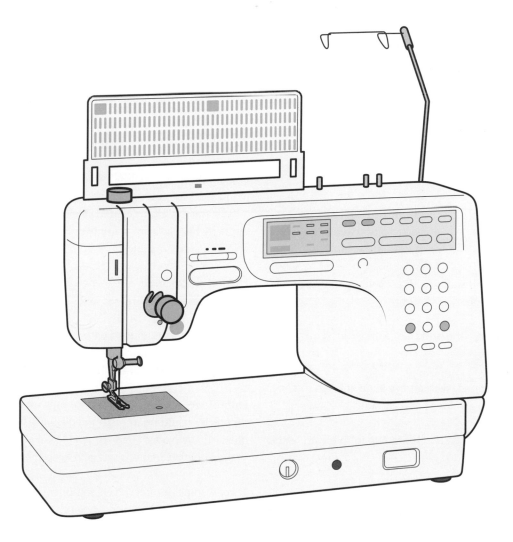

Users of computerized sewing machines can not only sew with increased precision and control but also change stitches at the touch of a screen and program their own settings, as well as reproduce past projects. And from a practical point of view, they benefit from the quick start/stop buttons, hands-free lifters for raising and lowering the presser foot, and automatic threaders and cutters.

Computerized machines contain microchips and several internal motors, which make them extremely versatile, although considerably more expensive than the standard electronic model

However, being such advanced pieces of sewing and embroidering equipment does not mean that they are beyond the capability of beginners. It is really a question of how much use one can make of such a huge range of stitches, fonts and functions.

It is wonderful to construct one's own designs with the built-in software or to be able to buy in from websites and download from a PC. Needleworkers can now operate on a different level from anything one could have imagined twenty or thirty years ago.

NEEDLES, PINS AND CUTTING TOOLS

Hand sewing needles are manufactured in a wide range of lengths and thicknesses; the higher the number the finer the needle. Decide on the best needle for the job from the following basic list:

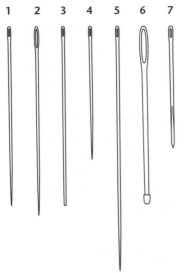

1 2 3 4 5 6 7

1 Sharps Medium-length and pointed, with a round eye, for general sewing with standard cotton or polyester thread.

2 Crewel or embroidery Pointed like sharps but with a long oval eye like a tapestry needle, for thicker or multiple threads.

3 Blunt-tipped Used for sewing knitted items, designed not to split the yarn.

4 Betweens Very short and sharp, with a small round eye. Used for fine stitching and quilting.

5 Milliners or straws Very long and thin, with a round eye, for decorative work and trims.

6 Bodkin Large, blunt-tipped, with an eye large enough to carry cord, elastic or ribbon through loops and casings.

7 Glovers or leather Sharp, with a 3-sided tip for piercing leather and PVC without tearing.

Most needles are nickel plated, although the quality varies. Gold- and platinum-plated needles don't discolour or rust but they are obviously more expensive. Keep and use a small emery cushion; the sand inside acts as an abrasive and polishes the needles and pins when they are pushed into it.

Pins made of hardened steel or brass will not rust; the smallest and finest are ideal for bridal and delicate fabrics. Coloured glass or plastic heads make pins easier to see and handle. Keep a large, flat-based pin cushion handy for general work; a small dressmaker's wrist cushion is also useful when you are busy fitting garments or soft furnishings.

Cutting tools (see p. 10)

Invest in the best quality shears and scissors that you can afford and don't allow anyone – including yourself – to blunt [dull] them by cutting paper, card, string or sticky tape. Look for blades secured with an adjustable screw rather than a rivet and have them professionally sharpened from time to time. Lefthanded scissors and shears are widely available through the internet.

Dressmakers' and tailors' shears have asymmetric handles and long blades for cutting smoothly through fabric at a low angle on a flat surface. Chrome-plated steel shears are the most durable but fairly heavy. There are lighter versions in stainless steel with coloured plastic handles.

Pinking shears make a scalloped or zigzag cut, producing a readymade seam finish that saves binding or oversewing.

Sewing scissors equipped with 15 cm [6 in] blades are the most useful size for your workbox. They have equal thumb and finger holes, and are used for trimming and clipping seams.

Embroidery scissors are used not only by embroiderers but for precision cutting in other needlecrafts such as tapestry and quilting. The blades are 3–10 cm [1¼–4 in] in length and so sharply pointed that it is safest to keep them in a case.

Thread snips [nippers] have self-opening spring-action blades, making them quick and convenient to use, as well as being extremely precise. Made of steel and also available in a nickel, chrome or Teflon finish, the blades measure about 11.5 cm [4½ in].

A **seam ripper**, as its name implies, is the most effective tool for opening seams and removing machine stitching. Use with care because it is all too easy to pierce the surrounding fabric.

THREAD

Choose a thread to suit your fabric so that sewing and laundering doesn't result in puckered seams, uneven shrinkage or broken fibres.

Silk thread (an animal fibre) is best for sewing woollens and silks. Cotton thread matches linen, cotton and rayon (all plant fibres); it has little 'give' in it and is always best used on a tightly woven fabric. By contrast, nylon (polyamide) and polyester threads stretch and recover well so they are suited to stitching synthetic and knit fabrics; polyester will also stitch wool. Button thread is a useful heavy-duty thread for coat buttons and craftwork.

Colourwise, if you cannot match thread to fabric exactly, go for a shade darker; for a woven tartan [plaid], choose thread to match the main colour.

Sewing threads are spun like knitting yarn by twisting two or more plys together; the tighter the twist, the smoother and stronger the thread will be. A loose twist produces a softer, lightweight thread like tacking [basting] cotton, which breaks more easily.

Twist goes from left to right (S twist) or from right to left (Z twist).

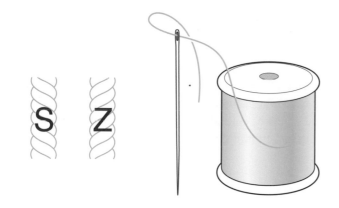

Standard sewing thread is spun with a Z twist, which makes it compatible with the workings of a lock-stitch sewing machine (pp. 16–17). Twist can also affect the way you thread a needle for hand sewing. Thread up with the free end as it comes off the reel [spool] and not only will it pass more easily through the eye of the needle, it won't tangle while you work.

Just like fabric and knitting yarns, sewing thread can be natural or man-made, or a combination of the two. Sewing with pure cotton has largely been replaced by cotton-covered polyester, where a polyester core provides strength and stretchability while the outer layer of mercerized cotton makes it smooth to work with.

We can still buy beautiful specialist threads of pure silk, linen, and even gold, which would have been familiar to needleworkers three or four hundred years ago. However, modern manufacturing processes have given us rayon or 'artificial silk' (1910), nylon (1935), polyester (1941) and aluminium metal fibre (1946) at far more modest prices. What's more, textile engineers continue to design and test new threads for ever-developing markets – such as protective work wear and sport and leisure clothing.

Although most modern threads will tolerate machine washing, drying and ironing, do bear in mind that some rayons can shrink in a hot wash, while nylon and metallic threads will melt in direct contact with a hot iron.

If you do a lot of hand sewing and want to work more quickly and smoothly, draw your thread across a block of beeswax (p. 10) to prevent it from getting tangled or frayed. The wax treatment works well in conditions of high humidity and will kill any static electricity from polyester fleece and similar synthetics.

Mercerized cotton has a finish applied to the plant fibres. They are immersed in sodium hydroxide (caustic soda) causing them to swell, untwist and shrink lengthwise. After rinsing, the fibres are left stronger, shinier and easier to dye.

FABRIC

Fabrics are manufactured from natural or man-made fibres, which are often mixed to combine their best qualities. For example, polyester cotton is equally comfortable but creases less than pure cotton; and the warmth of a woollen coat is complemented by the hard-wearing properties of nylon.

Woven fabric

There are three types of weave on which all woven fabrics are based: plain, twill and satin. Each has different properties. If you plan to sew your own clothes, it is a good idea to start with a firmly constructed lightweight material such as plain weave cotton.

1 **Plain weave** is the simplest type, where alternate warp (lengthwise) threads go over one and under one of the weft (crosswise) threads. Muslin, calico, taffeta and poplin are all familiar examples.

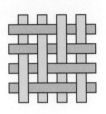

2 **Twill weave** interlaces warp and weft threads over and under two or more threads progressively. This produces a clear diagonal pattern on the surface of tough-wearing fabrics like drill, gabardine or denim.

3 **Satin weave** presents a smooth, compact surface created by long warp 'floats' (usually of silk, cotton, acetate or rayon) that leave no weft visible; the reverse is matt. If the floats are formed by the weft threads, the fabric is called 'sateen'. Either way, the glossy surface tends to snag.

The grain

The grain of a fabric is the direction in which the warp and weft threads lie. The warp runs lengthwise, parallel to the selvedge [selvage]: this is the *lengthwise grain*. The weft follows the *crosswise grain*, at right angles to the selvedge [selvage]. Check the grain before laying out a paper pattern (pp.20–21). For garments, it usually runs from shoulder to hem; for curtains, it should run lengthwise from top to bottom.

The bias

The bias lies along any diagonal line between the lengthwise and crosswise grains. True bias is at the 45 degree angle where you will get the maximum stretch. Strips cut on the bias are used for facings and bindings around necklines and armholes; they also form piping for soft furnishings.

Selvedge [selvage]

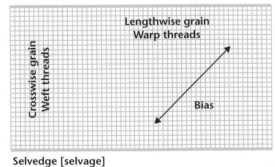

Selvedge [selvage]

Selvedge [selvage]

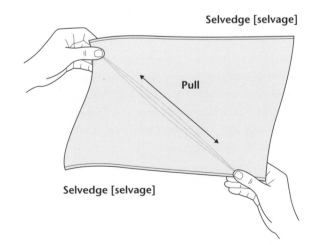

Pull

Selvedge [selvage]

Jacquard weave combines plain, twill and satin weaving to produce damasks, brocades and 'tapestries'. The technique was invented by Joseph Marie Jacquard in 1801, using a loom that wove intricate patterns controlled by a series of punched cards. Jacquard's revolutionary system later inspired mathematician Charles Babbage to develop the first mechanical computer.

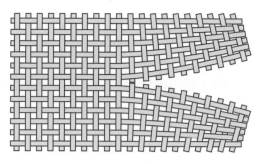

Tearing Of the three, the plain weave will tear most easily because its threads are close together and cannot take the strain by bending, stretching or twisting. Plain weave tears in a straight line along the grain.

Shrinkage The tighter the weave, the less likely a fabric is to shrink, both during and after manufacture. The shop label will tell you if a fabric is washable or 'dry clean only'. If it is not pre-shrunk you must do it yourself before cutting out. Immerse it in plain hot water for 30 minutes, then gently squeeze out, dry, and press if necessary.

Knit fabric

Knit fabric is made from interlocking looped stitches; this means cut edges won't unravel and the material does not crease readily. Knits are not always stretchy; a firm jersey or fleece fabric is quite stable. By contrast, knits containing spandex fibres stretch lengthwise and crosswise, making them perfect for dance and sportswear. There are two main types of knit: weft knitting and warp knitting (sometimes called 'raschel').

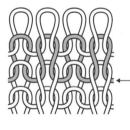

Weft thread 'course'

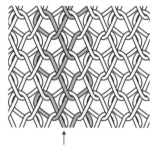

Warp thread 'wale'

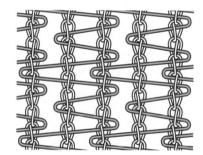

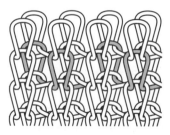

1 Weft knitted fabric is produced like hand knitting, with loops formed by working a single yarn in 'courses' or rows across the width of the fabric. It can be made on a variety of industrial or domestic knitting machines, and pieces can be shaped in the process. The 'course' construction means it can be unravelled from one loose end.

2 Warp knitting fabric is formed by multiple strands of yarn making loops vertically in individual 'wales' or columns. It uses a specialized machine to produce a fabric that stretches very little and won't ladder. Tricot and milanese for lingerie are typical products.

Warp-knitted end products include T-shirts, lace curtaining and blankets.

Raschel This type of warp knit has an open construction that can imitate lace and hand crochet, with heavy, textured inlaid threads held in place by a much finer yarn.

Interlock A smooth warp knit with closely interlocking stitches that allow it to stretch; it's typically used in the manufacture of underwear and casual clothes.

THE SEWING MACHINE

Your single most important item of sewing equipment, a well-built sewing machine – whether it's a cast iron heirloom or the latest computerized model – will give you decades of service so long as it is properly used and maintained.

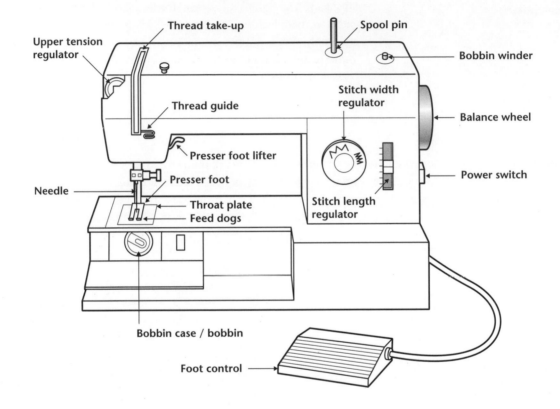

Buying new or secondhand, your choice will follow the kind of user you are. As a beginner or occasional sewer, look no further than a basic electric model (*shown above*) powered by an electric motor that drives the needle, bobbin and feed dogs, and operated by a foot pedal that controls sewing speed and fabric feed. It will sew different sizes of straight, hem, stretch and zigzag stitches selected at the twist of a dial, as well as button holes and a range of decorative stitches.

Computerized sewing machines (p. 11) are controlled by microchips and several internal motors, making them extremely

versatile and a good deal more expensive. Operated using a touchpad and LCD display, with or without a foot or knee pedal, these are sophisticated machines that will even warn you when the bobbin is running out.

The fact that they can memorize and reproduce past tasks and offer hundreds of different stitches via downloads from a PC indicates that they are best suited to regular and professional or semi-professional users. If you plan to create a lot of garments, run an alteration and repair service, make soft furnishings or do complex embroidery, they are a worthwhile investment.

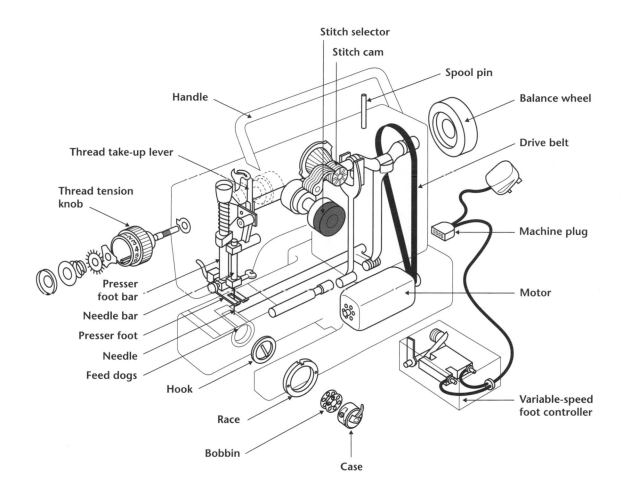

Stitch selector

Stitch cam

Handle

Spool pin

Balance wheel

Thread take-up lever

Drive belt

Thread tension knob

Machine plug

Presser foot bar

Needle bar

Presser foot

Motor

Needle

Feed dogs

Hook

Race

Bobbin

Case

Variable-speed foot controller

Prepare a list of the features that you want. Do you need a carrying case or will your machine be kept stationary on a table? Do you prefer a model with hand rather than foot control? Would you like it convertible from a flatbed to free arm access, which makes sewing sleeves easier?

Some basic requirements are: a good instruction manual; sturdy construction; bobbin is simple to wind and insert; threading up is straightforward; needles are easily changed; tension and pressure are adjustable; a lever or button for reverse stitching; variable speed control, including very slow; sews two or more layers of thick fabric without stalling; seam allowance marked on needle plate; light over needle area; thread cutter; minimal oiling, if any.

Garment-making on a large scale makes an overlocker [serger] worth considering. Widely used in industry, it combines machining, neatening and trimming seams in one operation. Overlockers operate with two, three or four threads producing looped stitches above and below the fabric edge; at the same time, a sharp cutter trims away the excess fabric.

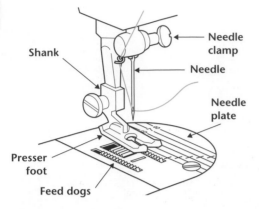

Shank

Needle
clamp

Needle

Needle
plate

Presser
foot

Feed dogs

Needle, presser foot, feed dogs, needle plate

General-purpose machine needles come in sizes 60–120 [8–19]. The finest will stitch delicates and the thickest will cope with tough fabrics like denim. Fit a ballpoint needle for knits or stretch fabrics. Needles will eventually go blunt [dull] or break, so keep some spare and change them frequently. The presser foot holds the fabric flat against the feed dogs while the needle makes the stitch. The feed dogs have tiny metal teeth that move the fabric from front to back as the stitching proceeds. The needle plate fits over the feed dogs, covering the bobbin, with a hole for the tip of the needle to pass through.

Machine feet

The shank of the foot (as seen on the straight-stitch foot below) attaches to the machine with a simple screw; newer machines have snap-on feet which save you time. There is a wide range of interchangeable feet, at least one for every stitch function. Here are five that form a useful basic kit.

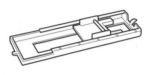

1 Straight-stitch The general purpose presser foot that comes ready to use on most machines.

2 Zigzag Has a horizontal slot to allow for the 'swing' of the needle as it forms a zigzag with the thread.

3 Zipper Used to insert zip fasteners and piping, or anywhere that the stitch line needs to run close. The foot can slide to left or right, and the needle operates in the tiny notch between the foot and the zip.

4 Walking/quilting Uses teeth to feed upper and lower layers of fabric together evenly and avoid bunching. Ideal for vinyl, velvets, big checks [plaids], and fabrics that tend to slip or stretch.

5 Buttonhole slide The button is placed in the carrier behind the needle and the stitching creates a buttonhole of the right length.

General care and maintenance

When not in use, all machines should have a cover: dust is a big enemy. Regularly clean under the feed dogs and around the bobbin race with a small brush – you will be surprised at the amount of fluff [lint] that gathers there. Oil the machine only according to the maker's instructions and run scrap cotton fabric through afterwards to soak up any excess. Avoid bent or broken needles by raising the needle high before removing work and don't drag on it while stitching. Sewing with a bent needle will cause it to hit the foot or needle plate and snap. Always raise the presser foot while threading the machine and lower it when you have finished work completely. As part of the power circuit, treat the foot control with care. Above all, switch power off before disconnecting any plugs or attempting cleaning or repairs.

Work at a table that is the right height for comfort and sit on an adjustable chair if possible. Facing a window will give the best light in the daytime. A pendant, standard or desk lamp can be used to direct extra light where you need it; fit daylight or halogen bulbs for a more natural effect.

PAPER PATTERNS

Taking measurements

1 Height Stand flat against a wall and measure from top of head to floor

2 Bust or chest Measure around the fullest part

3 Waist Measure around the natural waistline; do not pull tight

4 Hips Measure around the fullest part

5 Shoulders Measure across back from point to point of shoulders

6 Back–waist length Measure from nape of neck to waist

7 Sleeve length Measure from centre back neck, over point of shoulder and down slightly bent outer arm to wrist

8 Torso Measure from centre shoulder, under crotch, and back to shoulder

9 Inside leg Measure from crotch to instep on inner leg

10 Head Measure around widest part, across forehead

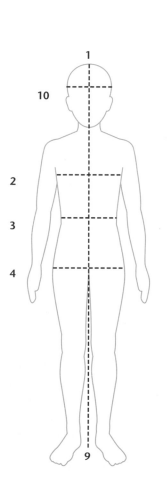

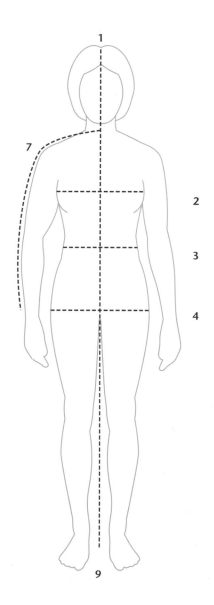

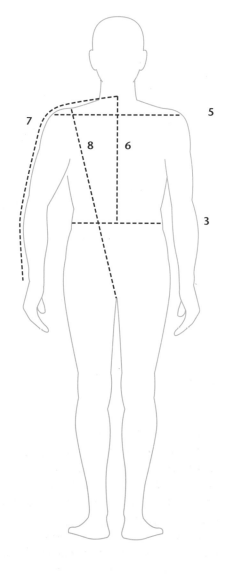

Anatomy of a paper pattern

The front of the pattern shows a colour illustration of the garment but the back of the envelope gives you all the essential information.

Body measurements and size chart →

SIZES/TAILLES	8	10	12	14	16	18	20	22	24
Bust	31½	32½	34	36	38	40	42	44	46
Waist	24	25	26½	28	30	32	34	37	39
Hip	33½	34½	36	38	40	42	44	46	48
Poitrine	80	83	87	92	97	102	107	112	117
Taille	61	64	67	71	76	81	87	94	99
Hanches	85	88	92	97	102	107	112	117	122

Style number →

X852   EASY/FACILE

Garment description →

MISSES' TUNIC, SKIRT AND PANTS: Pullover tunic A has collar, front facing, pockets and unfinished edges. Slim fitting skirt B and pants C sit 1" below waist and have concealed elastic waistlines.

Notions → **NOTIONS: Skirt B, Pants C:** 1½ yds. of 1" Elastic.

Suggested fabrics → **FABRICS: † Moderate Stretch Knits Only:** Lightweight Wool Jersey, Cotton Knit and Interlock. Unsuitable for obvious diagonals, plaids or stripes. Use nap yardages/layouts for pile, shaded or one-way design fabrics. *with nap. **without nap.

Combinations: BB(8-10-12-14), F5(16-18-20-22-24)

TUNIQUE, JUPE ET PANTALON (J. femme): Tunique à passer par la tête A avec col, parementure devant, poches et bord sans finition. Jupe B et pantalon C droits à 2.5 cm au-dessous de la taille, avec ligne de taille élastiquée cachée.

MERCERIE: Jupe B, Pantalon C: 1.4 m d'Elastique (2.5 cm).

TISSUS: † Uniquement pour tricot à élasticité moyenne: Jersey de laine fin, Tricot de coton et interlock. Rayures/grandes diagonales/écossais ne conviennent pas. Compte non tenu des raccords de rayures/carreaux. *avec sens. **sans sens.

Séries: BB(8-10-12-14), F5(16-18-20-22-24)

Meterage [yardage] required →

SIZES	8	10	12	14	16	18	20	22	24
TUNIC A 60"*	2	2⅛	2⅛	2⅛	2⅛	2⅛	2⅛	2⅛	2¼
SKIRT B 60"*, 7/8 yd.									
PANTS C 60"*	1¼	1¼	1¼	1¼	1⅜	1½	2⅛	2⅛	2¼

TAILLES	8	10	12	14	16	18	20	22	24
TUNIQUE A 150 cm*	1.9	2.0	2.0	2.0	2.0	2.0	2.0	2.0	2.1
JUPE B 150 cm*, 0.8 m									
PANTALON C 150cm*	1.2	1.2	1.2	1.2	1.3	1.4	2.0	2.0	2.1

Finished garment measurements →

Width, lower edge

	8	10	12	14	16	18	20	22	24
Tunic A	57½	58½	60	62	64	66	68	70	72
Skirt B	34	35	36½	38½	40½	42½	44½	46½	48½

Largeur, à l'ourlet

	8	10	12	14	16	18	20	22	24
Tunique A	146	149	152	157	163	168	173	178	183
Jupe B	87	89	93	98	103	108	113	118	123

Metric equivalents →

Width, each leg

	8	10	12	14	16	18	20	22	24
Pants C	16½	17	17½	18	18½	19	19½	20	20½

Largeur, chaque jambe

	8	10	12	14	16	18	20	22	24
Pantalon C	42	43	45	46	47	48	50	51	52

Back length from base of your neck

	8	10	12	14	16	18	20	22	24
Tunic A	29¾	30	30¼	30½	30¾	31	31¼	31½	31¾

Longueur – dos, votre nuque à l'ourlet

	8	10	12	14	16	18	20	22	24
Tunique A	76	76	77	78	78	79	80	80	81

Back length from waist
Skirt B, 26"

Longueur – dos, taille à ourlet
Jupe B, 66 cm

Side length from waist
Pants C, 42"

Longueur – côté, taille à ourlet
Pantalon C, 107 cm

Back view of garment →

FRONT DEVANT — A — A — B — B — C — C

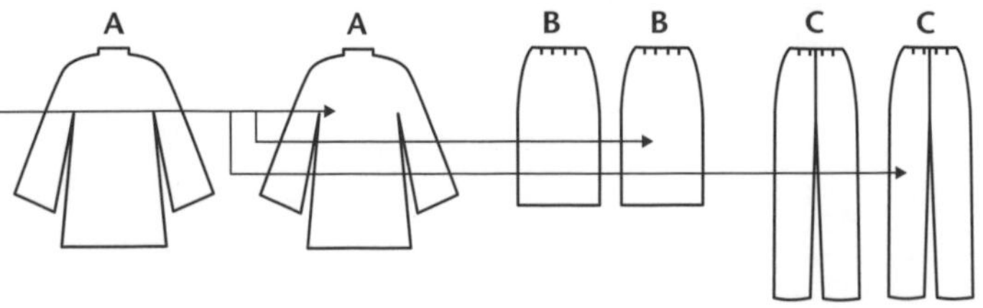

Inside the envelope you will find the printed pattern pieces together with the all-important sheet of directions. This sheet is a mini sewing tutorial, providing general instructions with explanations of pattern markings, the cutting layout, fabric preparation, a glossary of terms, and step-by-step sewing instructions.

A typical cutting layout is shown below. Fabric is manufactured in standard widths of 36–45 in (91–115 cm) for dress cottons; 52–60 in (137–152 cm) for polyester, wool, fleece and furnishing fabrics. Different layouts are provided for each width and whether the fabric has a directional nap like velvet, for example. Pattern shapes for interfacings and linings are included. The information is generally full and precise.

If you are working with a check [plaid] fabric, wide stripes or a large repeat design you may not be able to cut out pattern pieces economically and will probably need to buy extra fabric for matching seams and openings. This extra amount should be mentioned on the pattern; if not, ask the shop assistant for advice.

Cutting layout

The paper pattern pieces are arranged and pinned along the lengthwise grain of the fabric (pp. 14–15). The fabric is normally folded double but if a piece is to be cut from single thickness or on the crosswise grain it is clearly shown on the layout. The wrong side of the fabric is indicated by shading.

Pinning out is the stage at which you will take great care to match checks [plaids], stripes and any other important features of the fabric, such as shot silk or taffeta. A shot fabric has warp and weft [filling] in two different colours, so the fabric appears to change from one to the other at different angles.

If you need to mark your fabric – for example, to locate the position of darts or buttonholes – use tailor's chalk (p. 10) or any of the special fabric marker pens available. Some have water-soluble ink and some will simply fade after a day or two; always follow the maker's instructions for use. The pens are not usually recommended for 'dry clean only' fabric.

The notches on a paper pattern can either be cut out to stick up like a tab on the edge of the fabric or they can be cut the other way *into* the seam allowance, which is the reason they are called notches.

S/L stands for Selvedge [Selvage]/Lisiere; F/P stands for Fold/Pliure. The numbers refer to the different pattern pieces.

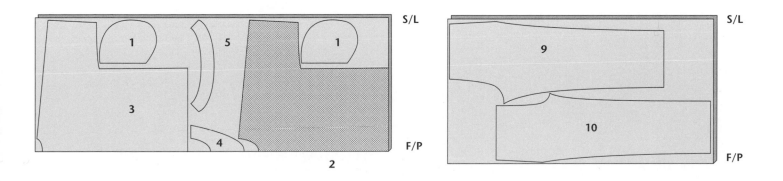

NOTIONS

Notions are all those extras required to make the garment, apart from the fabric itself. Listed below are some typical notions. Buy them at the same time as the fabric to ensure a good colour match if necessary.

A Thread

B Seam or bias tape

C Elastic

D Ribbon and lace

E Buttons

F Zip [zipper]

G Poppers/press studs [snaps]

H Hooks and eyes

I Hook and loop tape (Velcro)

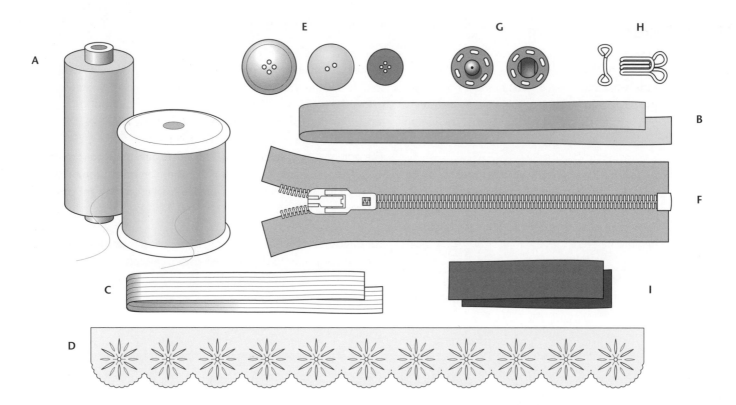

PART TWO:
HAND SEWING METHODS AND TECHNIQUES

THREADING A NEEDLE

If you have difficulty threading a needle for hand sewing, try using the needle threader that is supplied in sewing kits, or buy one from your haberdashery [fabric store].

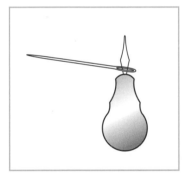

1 Holding the handle of the threader between thumb and forefinger, slide the empty wire loop through the eye of the needle.

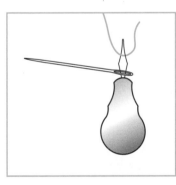

2 Place the sewing thread in the wire loop.

3 Pull the wire loop back through the eye of the needle, bringing the thread with it. Remove the wire loop by pulling through the short end of the thread until you have just one thread in the eye of the needle and the wire loop becomes free.

STRAIGHT SEWING STITCHES

Tacking [basting]

Holds fabric in position until final stitching is done. It's similar to running stitch but longer. Start with a knot, which you cut off when the time comes to remove the tacking [basting].

Running stitch

Simplest and most basic of stitches, used for seams and gathers. First secure thread with two small stitches on the spot. With needle at the front, push into fabric and out again in one move. Stitch and space should be of equal length. Fasten off with a back stitch.

Back stitch

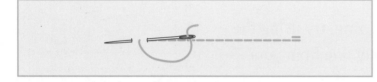

Imitates machine stitching. Begin exactly as for running stitch then stitch back over the first space. Needle out again at one stitch space ahead of the last stitch you made. Repeat with needle back in again at the point where the previous stitch ended.

Blanket stitch

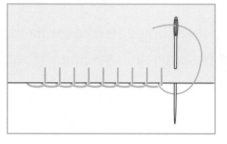

Used for neatening raw edges. Secured with a knot, bring needle through to front at stitch height and oversew fabric edge once, forming a loop. Pass needle through loop and pull tight against edge. Working from left to right, push needle into fabric again at same height. Pull needle forwards through new loop to form a half-hitch. Tighten as before. Repeat in a row and fasten off with extra half-hitch around final loop.

SEWING AN OPEN SEAM

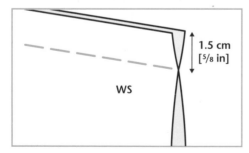

WS

1.5 cm
[⅝ in]

1 Pin and tack [baste] right sides together before stitching a line of running or back stitch 1.5 cm [⅝ in] from the edge of the fabric. This margin is called the *seam allowance*.

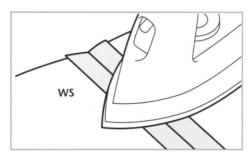

WS

2 Lay joined pieces out flat and press seam allowance open with an iron.

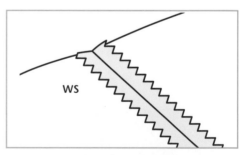

WS

3 Use pinking shears if necessary to neaten raw edges and prevent fraying. Alternatively, edges may be blanket-stitched or oversewn (p. 26).

SEWING AN ENCASED SEAM

Encased seams, such as the French seam, enclose allowances so that no raw edges are left visible. They are suitable for unlined garments, lingerie and sheer fabrics that tend to fray. The double stitching stands up well to frequent wear and washing.

Sewing a French seam by hand

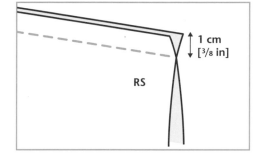

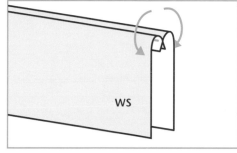

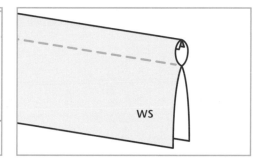

1 Pin and tack [baste] *wrong* sides together before stitching a line of running or back stitch 1 cm [³/₈ in] from the edge of the fabric.

2 Trim both layers of seam allowance to 3 mm [¹/₈ in] and fold right sides of the fabric together down the stitched line. Press along the fold, enclosing the trimmed seam allowance.

3 Stitch a second line 6 mm [¼ in] from fold and press the finished seam to one side.

CURVES AND CORNERS

Clipping outer and inner curves

Curved seams naturally give rise to curved seam allowances, which have to be clipped to allow them to stretch or fold together neatly and lie flat.

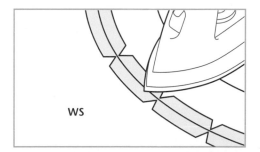

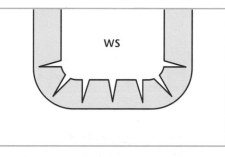

Necklines, armholes [armscyes] and pockets are all places where curves are clipped. If you have to clip down to the stitch line, be careful not to cut the stitching itself. If necessary afterwards, use the *tip* of the iron to press the seam open over a curved surface such as a ham (p. 10) or pressing mitt.

Single cuts at regular intervals may be enough to ease together silk or cotton lawn, but to avoid bulking up on thicker fabrics, cut wedge-shaped notches into the seam allowance and remove the excess completely.

Trimming corners

The same applies to corners, for example at the bottom of a bag or the ends of a waistband. Cut away excess fabric as close to the stitching as possible in order to turn out a sharp, right-angled corner. Use a crochet hook or knitting needle to help you – but nothing sharp that will damage the fabric.

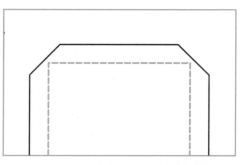

MENDING

Using straight stitches

Running stitch and back stitch are the ones to use for mending seams and casings (p. 28). Crossed seams – the point where four pieces of fabric are joined at the crotch or underarm of a garment – frequently need repair and to do this you must turn the garment inside out to reveal and replace the broken stitches. Begin and end 1 cm [³/₈ in] either side of the break, where the stitching is still good. Where a line of top stitching has given way on a casing or on a flat fell seam (p. 45) you will easily mend that from the right side. Always secure the repair thread at start and finish with a back stitch; knots put unnecessary strain on threads and will show through fine fabric when ironed.

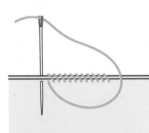 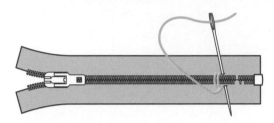 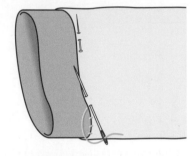

Oversewing

Used for sewing two neatened edges together, for example when mending a tear, or attaching a tie-belt or length of trim to a garment. First secure thread with two small stitches on the spot and carry on with neat diagonal stitches equally spaced. This stitch can be done from left to right or vice versa.

Oversewing a broken zip [zipper]

Provided the teeth are missing near the bottom of the zip [zipper] you can mend it by pulling the slider above the break and oversewing a new stop across both rows of teeth.

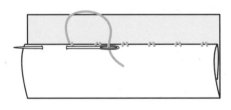

Slip stitch

Used for stitching a folded edge invisibly to a flat surface. Catch up a few threads of flat fabric with your needle, enter fold and slide along inside for up to 1 cm [³/₈ in] before coming out again to make the next stitch.

Repairing a sleeve lining

Slip stitch is ideal for repairing a sleeve lining at the cuff. If worn through, the lining can be completely undone around the inner cuff and turned up to hide the worn section. Pin the new fold and slip stitch the lining back into place.

USING A SEAM/HEM GAUGE

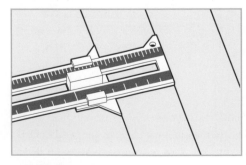

This is a 15 cm [6 in] gauge fitted with a sliding marker that allows you to set it on a fixed measurement. Use to ensure an even seam allowance or hem, or to measure pleats and buttonholes accurately.

HEMMING

Turning a hem

Hemming is frequently done by hand, even when the rest of a garment is machine stitched.

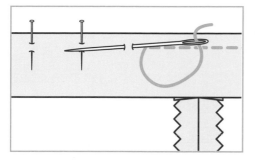 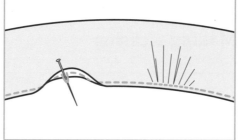 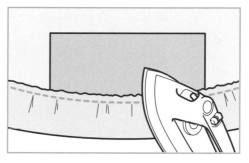

1 Let the garment hang for a day before pinning up the hem, then tack [baste] the lower edge and turn the raw edge over at the top, ready to stitch. If the fabric is fraying or too thick, sew tape around the right side of the raw edge and hem stitch on to that (p. 30).

2 For a flared or circular hem, ease fullness with running stitch around the top edge. Pull up regular groups of gathers using a pin, then tack [baste] in preparation for stitching. Alternatively, attach bias tape (p. 30) after gathering.

3 Steam pressing heavy woollen fabric helps to reduce hem fullness. Use cloth or thick paper to avoid making a ridge on the front of the fabric. Press very lightly and lift the iron clear – never drag it across damp fabric.

Hemming stitch

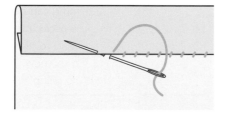

The second turn of the hem should be narrower than the first, about 7–10 mm [¼–³⁄₈ in]. Secure thread with two small stitches on the edge of this fold. Begin hemming by picking up two or three threads of the main fabric before passing needle up to catch the fold again. This stitch can be worked from right or left.

Slip hemming

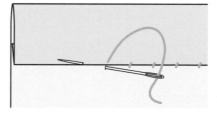

Similar to slip stitch (p.26). Pick up a few threads of fabric with the needle, enter fold and slide along inside for up to 1 cm [³⁄₈ in] before emerging to make the next stitch.

Herringbone (Catchstitch) flat hem

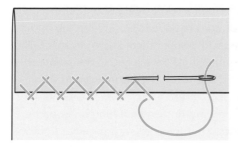

Secures hems on thick, non-fraying fabrics where no second turning is made. It is basically a large cross stitch formed by making a back stitch alternately in each layer of fabric.

Rolled hem

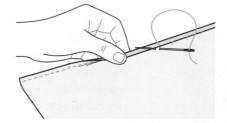

For delicate fabrics: first stitch along a marked hemline with a fine needle. Trim to within 5 mm [¼ in] of that line and, between thumb and forefinger, start rolling the raw edge over the stitching. Insert your needle through the roll, catch a thread or two in the main fabric and slide the needle into the roll again. Every few stitches, draw up thread to secure roll.

CASINGS

A casing is a tube for elastic, cord or ribbon. Stretch waistbands, scrunchies and shoebags all use casings. In home furnishing, the casing may take a curtain rod or wire. Make it deep enough and you can stitch a second line to hold the rod *and* create a frilled curtain top.

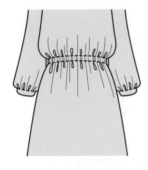

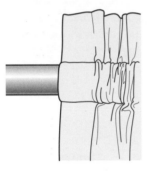

Making a casing

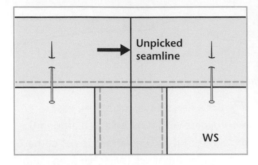

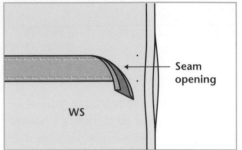

1 Fold fabric over twice, like a hem. Pin, then stitch. If hand sewing, use back stitch for strength because a casing gets considerable wear. To leave a gap for drawstrings (on a shoebag, for example) unpick both side seams above the horizontal stitch line; leave the seam allowance turned inside.

2 Alternatively, create a channel with straight tape. Sewn on to the wrong side of the fabric, it should be a little wider than the elastic, ribbon or cord going through it. Make use of any seam openings to thread the elastic etc., but close them separately without blocking the channel.

Threading the casing

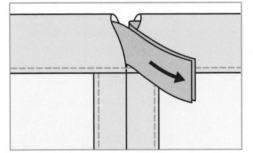

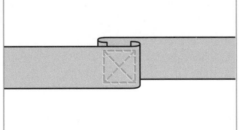

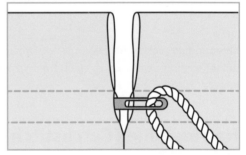

1 Calculate how much elastic you need by stretching it around the waist, wrist etc. and allow extra for adjustment and sewing the ends. It will be shorter than the casing, so safety-pin the free end to the fabric before threading; the casing will gather up as you go. Level the ends outside the casing when threading is done, pin together and check for fit.

2 Trim any excess if necessary, then join the elastic as shown, unless it is very narrow and you are unable to fold the ends. Stitch a square and/or a cross for a really firm hold. The waistband, cuff etc. can then be closed.

3 To fit a two-way drawstring, buy enough cord to go twice round the top of the bag with about 30 cm [12 in] to spare. The casing should have a gap in the seam on each side. Cut the cord in half and with a bodkin, thread each half right around the casing, starting and finishing on opposite sides. Knot the cord ends together tightly; pull both sides at once to close the bag.

PROJECT: DRAWSTRING FAVOUR BAG

This little bag measures 10 x 18 cm [4 x 7 in] and can be hand sewn using organza and ribbons to hold favours for parties, weddings or naming ceremonies. Made from muslin or fine cotton lawn, it could also contain a sachet of lavender or aromatic cedar wood for a clothes cupboard or drawer. The same pattern may be scaled up to the appropriate size for laundry, shoes or toys, using any suitable fabric.

To make a favour bag, you will need:
• a piece of organza cut to 13 x 46 cm [5¼ x 18 in]
• a 25 cm [10 in] length of silk, satin or nylon ribbon 15 mm [⅝ in] wide for the external casing
• 65 cm [26 in] of matching ribbon 7 mm [¼ in] wide for the two-way drawstring. Alternatively, use the same amount of thin silky cord

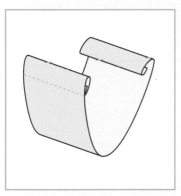

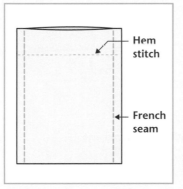

Hem stitch

French seam

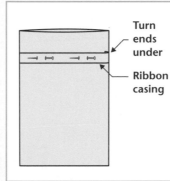

Turn ends under

Ribbon casing

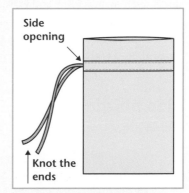

Side opening

Knot the ends

1 Fold over 5 cm [2 in] on each end of the fabric and slip hem the turnings as shown on p. 27. Fold the hemmed fabric in half with the wrong sides facing.

2 Make an encased seam on each side of the bag, following the instructions on p. 25. When the French seams are done, turn the bag right side out, ready to apply the ribbon casing to the outer surface.

3 Cut the casing ribbon in half. Take one piece, turn raw ends under and pin across one side of the bag, concealing the line of hem stitches. Create a channel with small, even running stitches (p. 24) along each edge. Repeat and match with the remaining ribbon on the other side.

4 There will be a narrow opening in the casing on either side of the bag, level with the side seams. Cut the drawstring ribbon or cord in half and use a bodkin or small safety pin to thread it right around the casing (see instructions opposite). Knot the ends together. With remaining ribbon or cord, repeat from the opposite side.

Place the favour inside the bag and draw up the ribbons or cord to close it. Before you fill the bag, you might like to trim it in various ways, with embroidery, lace or beads.

BINDING

There are two main types of binding tape, although they are available in different materials, from heavy duty twill to nylon net.

Straight tape

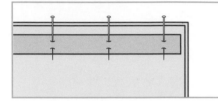

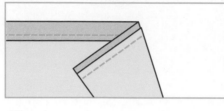

1 Straight tape is used to reinforce the stitching on seams where there may be too much tension on the sewing thread alone, such as shoulders and waistbands. The tape is pinned over the stitch line so that the stitching will go through three layers all together.

2 When the seam is done, the seam allowance is trimmed back close to the stitch line without cutting into the tape.

3 Straight tape is also useful for turning hems. If the fabric is thick or fraying, sew tape around the right side of the raw edge and use it as the hemming edge.

Bias binding

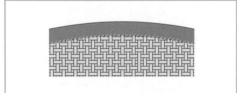

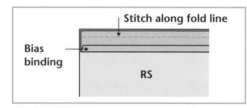

1 Bias binding, as its name implies, is manufactured on the bias (p. 14) and follows the contours of any seam. It is used to encase fraying edges, particularly on thick fabrics and quilted items that cannot be neatened by turning.

2 Press one half of the bias binding open, align with the raw edge of the fabric on the *right* side and stitch along the fold line of the binding (for speed, if possible use a sewing machine for this).

3 Fold binding over the raw edge to meet the previous line of stitches on the wrong side. Slip stitch along fold of binding.

Bias binding as decoration

Bias binding is frequently used decoratively and can be bought in many colours and patterns. It is made in satin as well as matt finish and in a range of widths. For true originality, make your own bias binding from any fabric so long as it is cut properly at an angle of 45 degrees to the grain. To use as double fold tape you must cut the strip four times the planned finished width.

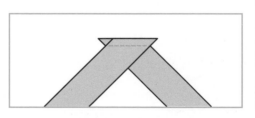

1 Joining the strips is managed by stitching along the straight grain with the bias strips at a right angle. Press the seam flat open afterwards.

2 Binding the edge of a baby's bib not only solves the problem of hemming towelling fabric, but the binding can also be extended to form the neck ties.

GATHERING AND PLEATING

Both gathers and pleats are designed to deal with the fullness of fabric.

Gathers

Casings (p. 28) are an adjustable means of gathering – as is rufflette tape on curtains – but we need to fix gathers permanently too, for example on a gathered skirt or puffed sleeve.

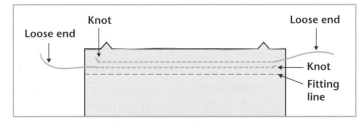

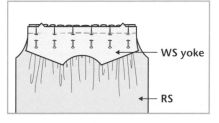

1 Within the seam allowance of 1.5 cm [⁵⁄₈ in], sew two lines of evenly spaced running stitch in opposite directions. Start each with a strong knot and leave the far end loose.

2 The gathers will draw up when both loose ends are gently pulled at the same time. Wind each end around a pin to keep fabric to the desired width.

3 Lay the gathers out flat and adjust if necessary before pinning on the yoke or waistband and tacking [basting] ready for final stitching. This is the time to add straight tape reinforcement if required (see opposite).

Pleats

Pleats regulate fullness in a more structured way than gathers. They need careful measurement and a lot of preparation in terms of pinning and tacking [basting]. Have the steam iron ready because pleating demands that you press as you go.

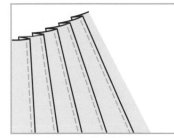

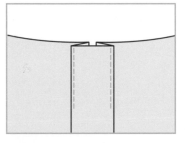

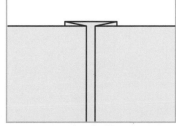

1 A knife pleat is a simple fold in one direction only, either left or right. Pressing the pleats will set them but thicker fabrics are often edge stitched too, to keep a sharper outline.

2 A box pleat is formed by two knife pleats facing opposite ways. These are usually top stitched to help maintain their shape around the hips.

3 An inverted box pleat is made when the knife pleats point in towards each other. This is a common feature of pockets on military uniforms.

A kick pleat is a short, closed pleat, usually about 30 cm [12 in] long, at the hem of a straight skirt, usually at the back. It allows greater freedom of movement and must be reinforced at the top on either side to prevent tearing.

SMOCKING

Smocking is a traditional form of hand embroidery, worked over small folds of evenly gathered fabric. When the gathering threads are removed the resulting fabric is quite stretchy, which is ideal for children's clothes. Smocking also looks good on the yoke area of blouses and around the cuffs of full sleeves, and it makes an attractive pocket detail. In the realms of home furnishings, panels of smocked silk, linen or velvet look luxurious on cushion [pillow] covers. It takes extra fabric – on average allow three to four times the intended final width.

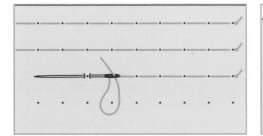

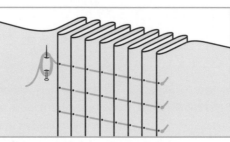

Now you can begin embroidering across the fronts of the folds. Standard six-strand embroidery cotton [floss] is suitable – although you will work with only three strands at a time – and a crewel or embroidery needle (p. 12).

1 Unless you are smocking a gingham or stripe, where the pattern provides a guide, you will have to iron a transfer of smocking dots on to the *wrong* side of your fabric and *with the grain*. Stitch between the dots as shown, using contrasting thread that will be easy to remove.

2 Pull up the gathering threads – not too tightly – and tie in pairs or wrap around pins to keep your fabric to the desired width. Make sure the gathers are even.

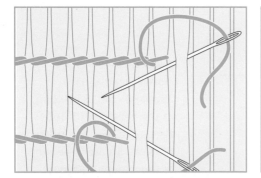

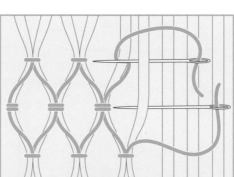

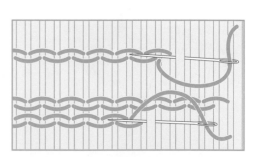

1 **Stem stitch** Because smocking is meant to be fairly elastic, try not to work too tightly. Make your first row in this simple stitch to test and establish your tension.

2 **Surface honeycomb stitch** Back stitch across two folds, needle out between them, go down 6 mm [¼ in] and enter the next right-hand fold from right to left. Make another back stitch at that point and repeat the sequence going up and down alternately. Repeat a line below, mirrorwise, to form the honeycomb pattern. Always check thread is correctly above or below needle.

3 **Cable stitch** Needle out through first fold left, thread below needle and stitch over second fold, bringing needle out between first and second. Work with thread above and below needle alternately. Double cable stitch is two rows of cable worked together so they reflect each other.

WAISTBANDS AND CUFFS

Waistbands have to be firm and so they are usually cut out in the warp direction (p. 14) parallel to the selvedge [selvage]. They can be supported by a very stiff tape like Petersham, which remains visible on the inside of the band. A flat skirt or trouser hook may be incorporated into the overlapping end, with a bar to match on the other end.

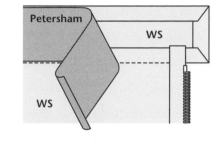

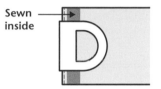

Alternatively, waistbands – and cuffs – can be strengthened internally with a material such as buckram or vilene. Some interfacings are iron-on, which can save you time but you should check machine washability.

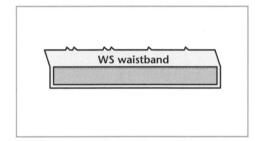

1 Fold waistband in half lengthwise and stitch interfacing into position against centre line.

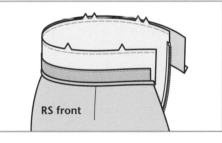

2 Match pattern notches, pin and tack [baste] right sides together and firmly stitch waistband to skirt (if possible use a sewing machine for this). Press up the narrow turning below the interfacing.

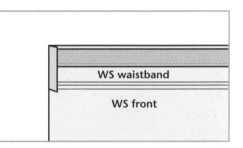

3 Trim and layer seam allowances to reduce bulk before they are encased.

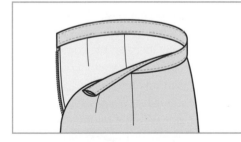

4 Fold waistband along edge of interfacing so that pressed-up edge meets main stitch line. Pin, tack [baste] and hem to finish.

The hook-and-loop system of fastening known as Velcro needs very little pressure and is ideal for anybody who finds buttons and zip fasteners difficult to manage. Velcro can be trimmed to size without fraying and sewn in position as required on cuffs and waistbands and plackets. Take care to seal all Velcro surfaces before putting in the washing machine.

OPENINGS AND FASTENINGS

Below every waistband or collar lies the opening. The simplest kind is where the seam turnings are neatened with a tape insert. A more substantial opening contains a placket. This two-strip placket is neatly constructed from two pieces of fabric, one single and one folded double. It is an opening that could take a zip [zipper] (p. 47) just as easily as a row of buttons or a strip of Velcro. Note the topstitched reinforcement.

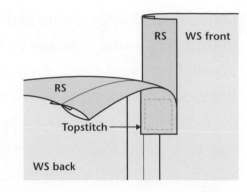

Fastenings

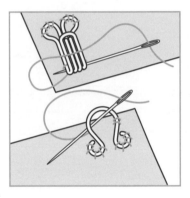

1 Use one or two hook and eye combinations to fasten a waistband, depending on the width. Waistbands take a lot of stress, so work buttonhole stitch around the hook and eye attachments, with additional oversewing to prevent them loosening.

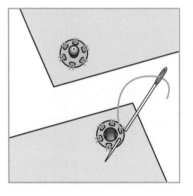

2 Using all four holes, sew the stud half of the popper [snap] to the overlap so that it presses home more effectively. Don't let the stitches show on the right side. Line up the position for the lower half by running your needle through the centre hole of the stud. If desired, sew a button on the right side of the overlap directly over the stud.

Sewing on a coat button

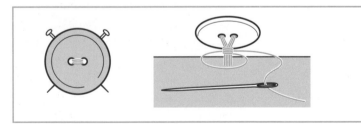

Use double sewing thread if you have no button thread. Buttons on coats and jackets should not be sewn tight against the cloth but should allow room for an extra layer when done up. Some buttons are manufactured with a shank but many are not. The thickness of two pins criss-crossed beneath the button will establish the shank's length and after a few stitches you can remove the pins and start to wind the thread around it. Finish with a row of buttonhole stitches for extra strength.

Sewing a button loop

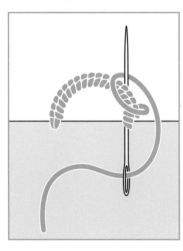

Loops make good alternative fastenings for clothes and bags. Sew them on the edge of one side, to align with a toggle or button on the other. Secure thread by oversewing, test for size with the button and loop across to a second fixing point. Continue looping to and fro several times before buttonhole stitching neatly to hold the strands together.

MAKING A HAND-SEWN BUTTONHOLE

Once you know how many buttons you will be using, you must decide whether the buttonholes will run vertically or horizontally and how far from the edge. The answer depends on the direction of strain that the button(s) will take. If there is none, the holes can be made vertical, since the button does not need to move at all.

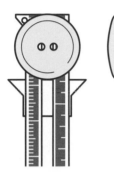

The finished buttonhole should not be over 3 mm [1/8 in] longer than the button itself but you have to make an initial cut in the fabric. As a rule, add the width of the button to its thickness, plus the 3 mm [1/8 in] for ease. Testing first on a spare scrap of fabric, mark the length with a pin at each end and tack [baste] or draw an accurate line between the two. Using very sharp embroidery scissors or a seam ripper, pierce the fabric mid-line and cut.

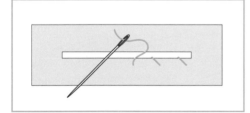

1 Overcast the cut edges to prevent them fraying. Make four to six stitches down each side of the buttonhole. They should be about 3 mm [1/8 in] deep.

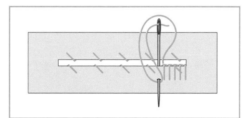

2 Hold the buttonhole as flat as possible while you are sewing. Buttonhole stitch is the same as blanket stitch (p. 24) but the stitches lie much closer together. Keep them the same depth for neatness.

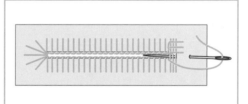

3 This style of buttonhole is called *fan and bar* due to the shapes the stitches make at either end. You may choose to make both ends the same. The 'bar' is said to be stronger because of the two or three straight stitches that form the foundation for the buttonhole stitches that cover them. The 'fan' is more attractive and consists of five graded stitches with the longest in line with the cut.

ATTACHING SET-IN SLEEVES

There are many different styles of sleeve, for example (*from left to right*): raglan, dolman, bishop, puffed, tucked and tailored. Notice that neither raglan nor dolman styles have an over-shoulder seam – they are not 'set-in' like the others.

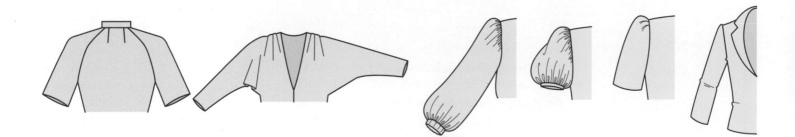

The set-in sleeve is joined to the main garment by a seam that goes all the way round the armhole [armscye]. Whether gathered or tailored, the set-in sleeve demands the most preparation by hand, although the final stage is usually machine sewn. The process begins with cutting out and it is immediately obvious that the sleeve head is larger than the armhole [armscye] it is intended for. However, it is the cut of the sleeve head that enables the arm to move freely.

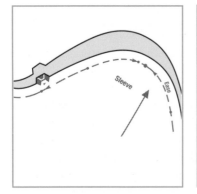

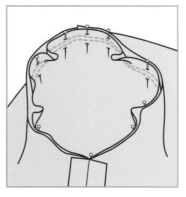

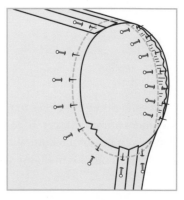

1 The sleeve pattern has notches that correspond to those on the armhole [armscye] of the main garment, and also markings to show the extent of the gathering line within the curve of the sleeve head.

2 Sew a double line of running stitches along the gathering line, leaving the thread ends free. Afterwards, join the sleeve seam, press it open and turn sleeve right side out.

3 Pin the head into the armhole [armscye] before pulling up to fit. Pull the gathers evenly and the head will smooth out. For a puffed sleeve rising above the shoulder seam, pull the outer line more than the inner one to make the sleeve head arch over.

4 Distribute the gathers evenly, but *do not cut away any excess fabric yet*. Tack [baste] firmly and remove the pins before trying the garment on. Now is the time for any alterations. A tailored sleeve should be smooth-fitting with no puckering on the right side. After final stitching, neaten armhole [armscye] by oversewing or binding.

TRIMMING: BEADS, SEQUINS AND BOWS

Beads

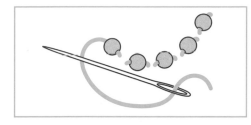
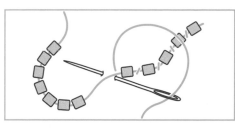
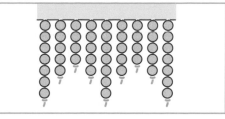

Choose the correct size and shape of beads for your design and work with a fine needle. Secure thread, bring needle through and thread on one bead. Insert needle back into or near the same hole. Advance one stitch on wrong side and bring needle through ready for next bead.

Thread up two needles and secure both threads on the wrong side. Bring first needle through and thread with desired number of beads. With second needle, stitch over the first thread coming through the first bead; this is *couching*. Slide the second bead close to the first and repeat until all beads are in place.

For a bead fringe, tie first (anchor) bead on to thread and knot firmly. Add as many beads as desired, securing thread with two small stitches on the fabric edge before finishing off. Start a new strand in the same way, next to the first.

Sequins

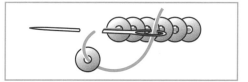

Secure thread on wrong side and bring needle up through eye of first sequin. Back stitch over the right hand edge, come out on the left hand edge and back stitch down through the eye. Advance a stitch and repeat with next sequin.

Secure thread on wrong side and bring needle up through eye of first sequin. Thread on one small bead before re-inserting needle through same eye. Pull firmly to bring bead in contact with sequin. Advance one stitch on wrong side and bring needle up through eye of next sequin.

To overlap sequins, secure thread on wrong side and bring needle up through eye of first sequin. Needle in on left hand edge and up again at distance of half a sequin. Thread second sequin on and back stitch to edge of first one. Advance one stitch on wrong side and bring needle up again at distance of half a sequin. Each new sequin covers the eye of the previous one.

Flat ribbon bow

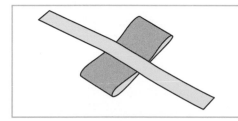
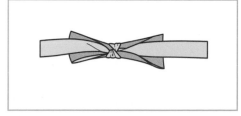

1 Take two lengths of ribbon, one wide and one narrow. Loosely fold the wide one into a rectangle with ends overlapping halfway down the longer side. Join three layers together with a small cross stitch and lay the narrow ribbon across at right angles.

2 Turn both ribbons over and tie the narrow one in a knot that will pinch the wide ribbon into a bow shape.

3 Turn the ribbons right side up. Pull both ends of the narrow ribbon so they hang one side of the wide one. Trim level.

PROJECT: APRON

This apron has a large double pocket, useful for cooks, gardeners and craftspeople. Make it from any close woven, pre-shrunk fabric like canvas, denim, calico or gingham.

Make a paper pattern by ruling a large sheet of paper with a grid of 5 cm [2 in] squares. Scale up the pieces, square by square, from the grid below; a 1.5 cm [5/8 in] seam allowance has been included all round. Cut out the paper shapes and pin to the fabric; remember to place the centre of the main piece on a fold. Cut out the fabric and remove the paper.

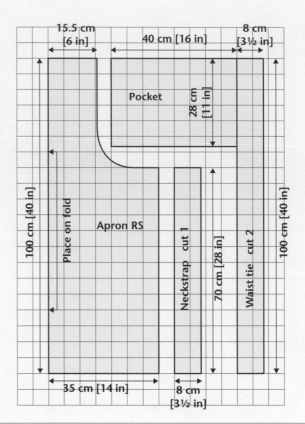

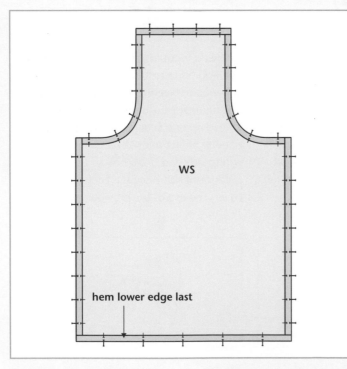

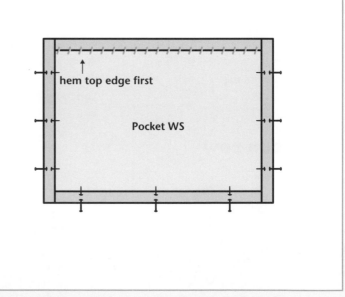

1 Fold over and pin 1.5 cm [5/8 in] in a neat hem around the main piece; clip the waistline curves for a smooth turning. Tack [baste] and then machine or hem stitch right round, finishing along the lower edge. Press.

2 Hem the top of the pocket piece. With a single fold, tack [baste] down the seam allowance on the other three sides. Press. If you like, add an appliquéd or embroidered design to the pocket at this stage.

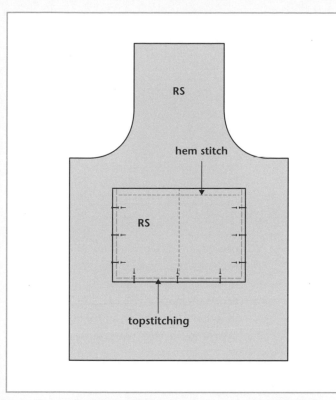

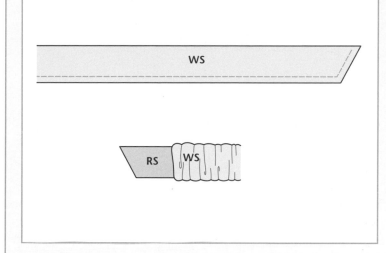

4 Fold the neck strap and waist ties in half lengthwise, RS together. Stitch one end and the side seams on all three, as shown. Clip the points and corners, turn RS out and press.

3 Pin the pocket on to the RS front of the apron piece, at hip level. Tack [baste] and topstitch into place. Topstitch the centre line of the pocket first, to prevent puckering, then finish around the edges.

5 For an adjustable neck strap, make three buttonholes. Turn in the raw end of the strap and neaten by oversewing. Attach it to one corner of the apron top with reinforced stitching, as shown. Sew a button to the other corner. Alternatively, you may make one buttonhole in the apron top and sew three buttons to the strap.

6 Finish the waist ties in the same way as the neck strap, minus the buttonholes.

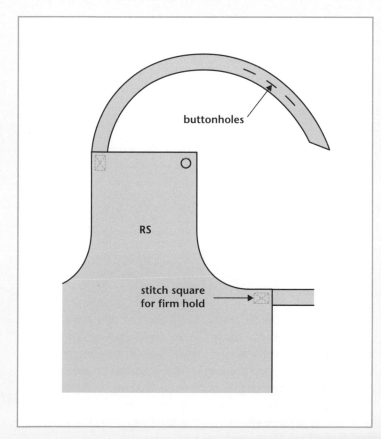

TRIMMING: EDGINGS, ROULEAU AND APPLIQUÉ

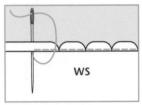

Shell edging
Fold or roll and tack a narrow double turning. Make a decorative hem with three running stitches followed by a vertical loop up over the edge. Pull tight to form the scallop. If necessary, make two vertical stitches, depending on fabric thickness.

Lace edging
Tack [baste] a narrow turning, then pin and tack [baste] a length of gathered lace behind the fold. Sew all three layers together with neat running or back stitch; alternatively, use a straight machine stitch.

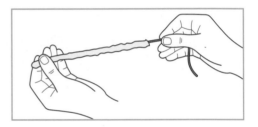

Faggoting Lay lace parallel to fabric and tack [baste] both on to backing paper. Bring needle through lower edge and insert into top edge from back to front a little to the right. Twist needle under and over thread across the gap, then insert into lower edge from back to front, again to the right. Repeat to the end, remove paper.

Rouleau

1 Rouleau is constructed from bias strips (p. 30). It is used to make spaghetti straps; stitched-down designs on lapels and bodices; and wired trimmings for hats and bridal head-dresses.

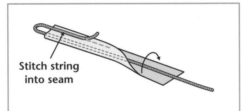

Stitch string into seam

2 Fold bias strips right sides together, and sew to the required width. Stretch fabric slightly as you go so it won't strain the thread later. Include a length of thin string, longer than the tube, at the top of the seam and push the free end down inside. Finish stitching the seam.

3 Trim the seam allowance to 3–6 mm [1/8–1/4 in]. Pull on the string to turn the tube right side out. Pull slowly at first until you feel the fabric coming through.

Appliqué

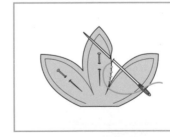

1 Appliqué is cut-out fabric decoration attached to a base by stitching around the shapes. It is used in dressmaking and home furnishings, especially quilts. First cut out pieces with a small seam allowance, snip any curves (p. 25) and pin or tack [baste] them to the base fabric, with guidelines if necessary.

2 With a straw needle, stitch down the shapes, turning the raw edges in with the needle as you go; use hemming (p. 27) or blanket stitch (p. 24). Appliqué by machine offers a wide choice of stitch effects.

3 Remove pins and tacking [basting] when you have finished. Press your appliqué lightly, face down on a well-padded surface like a towel, so the seam allowances don't show through on the front.

PART THREE:
MACHINE SEWING METHODS AND TECHNIQUES

THREADING THE SEWING MACHINE

Newer-style sewing machines incorporate the tension discs, thread guides and take-up lever inside their casings, eliminating various steps involved with threading the older models. We include both because many older machines are still in use (see also pp. 16–17). If possible, *consult the manufacturer's manual* but here are general instructions for preparing the top thread on a sewing machine.

1 Lift the presser foot to release tension discs and allow thread to run easily.

2 Raise needle as far as possible by turning the hand/balance wheel.

3 Place a reel of thread on the spool pin and pull the free end into the first thread guide.

4 On new-style machines, take thread around the auto tension channel and down to the thread guide just above the needle. On older models, thread around the tension dial and snap up through the tension wire.

5 Older models also operate with a prominent take-up lever. Pass the thread through the eye of this lever and then down to the thread guide just above the needle.

6 Now thread the needle. Be aware that some thread from front to back and some from left to right. Look for the groove above the eye where the thread runs during stitching. Finally, pull through a good working length of thread, about 15 cm [6 in].

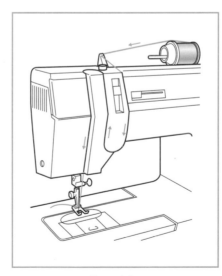

New style

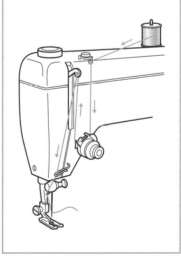

Old style

Incorrect threading is probably responsible for more beginners' problems than any other factor. If you have no book of instructions, search for your make and model on the internet, where a huge range of manuals is available.

THE BOBBIN

The bobbin holds the lower thread on a sewing machine. It lies next to the needle plate, in a compartment with a sliding lid. Lower thread tension is controlled by a small screw that regulates the spring on the bobbin case. Some bobbins operate clockwise and others anticlockwise – once again, *consult the manufacturer's manual.*

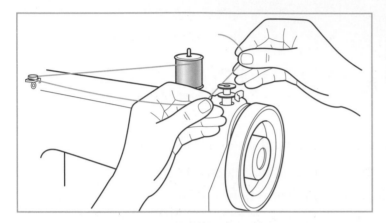

The bobbin is filled automatically from the winder on the machine, which ensures it is evenly wound under tension. Some bobbins can be filled in situ under the plate.

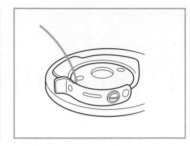

This type sits vertically in the bobbin race and is released by a latch on the case. When replaced, the thread should slot under the spring with a tail of 10 cm [4 in].

The 'drop-in' type sits horizontally beneath the lid. There is usually an angled slot to pull the bobbin thread through.

THE IMPORTANCE OF TENSION

The machine stitch is formed by the top and lower threads interlocking in the fabric.

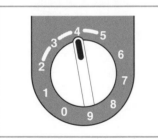

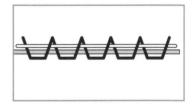

1 Top thread tension is governed by the tension dial, numbered 0–9. Behind it, the thread runs between two or three discs that are adjusted according to the dial.

2 Between 4 and 5 on the dial is considered 'normal' tension. The threads meet in the centre of the fabric and the stitching appears the same on each side.

3 Below 4, the tension discs loosen and the top thread runs more freely. The thread can then pass through both layers of fabric. This is only desirable if you want to create gathers by pulling up the bottom thread.

4 Above 5, the discs are screwed together more tightly and the reverse happens.

TROUBLESHOOTING

PROBLEM	REASON	REMEDY
Machine does not sew	Power switch is turned off	Turn on the switch
	Bobbin winder is engaged	Disengage bobbin winder
Fabric does not move	Presser foot is not lowered	Lower presser foot
Machine skips stitches	Machine is not threaded correctly	Re-thread correctly
	Needle blunt or loose	Change needle and tighten
Needle unthreads	Needle wrong way round	Set needle correctly
Needle breaks	Bent needle	Change needle. Raise needle when removing work
Stitches are irregular	Needle size is not correct for thread and fabric	Use appropriate needle
	Machine is not threaded correctly	Re-thread correctly
	Top thread tension is too loose	Adjust tension
	Fabric is being pulled or pushed against machine	Guide gently with feeding action
Puckered seams	Tension too tight or needle wrong way round	Loosen top tension or set needle correctly
Thread breaks	Tension too tight or needle wrong way round	Loosen top tension or set needle correctly
Snagged fabric	Bent or blunt needle	Change needle
Thread bunches	Top bobbin threads are not drawn back under	Draw both threads back under presser foot before starting seam about 10 cm [6 in] and hold until a few stitches are formed
Bobbin thread breaks	Bobbin case is not threaded correctly	Check bobbin is rotating in the right direction
Lint accumulates in bobbin case or hook		Remove lint
Tangled bobbin thread	Bobbin wound too loosely or inserted wrongly	Do not wind bobbins by hand. Check bobbin unreels in the right direction

STITCH LENGTH

Stitch length is now measured in millimetres from 1 to 6 and controlled by a dial or lever (pp. 16–17). This activates the feed dogs, which in turn move fabric the required distance under the pressure foot (p. 18).

Use the longest stitches (4–6 mm [$\frac{1}{8}$–$\frac{1}{4}$ in]) for heavyweight fabrics, topstitching, gathering and tacking [basting]. Medium length stitches (2.5–4 mm [$\frac{3}{32}$–$\frac{1}{8}$ in]) are suitable for mid-weight fabrics. Fine fabrics use a 2 mm [$\frac{1}{16}$ in] stitch. A row of 1 mm [$\frac{1}{32}$ in] stitches is difficult to unpick, so it pays to be sure of what you are doing when using them.

STITCH WIDTH

Stitch width does not apply to straight stitching. The width control (pp. 16–17) sets the 'swing' of the needle when working zigzag or other decorative stitches. Again, the measurement is in millimetres and usually goes up to 6 mm [$\frac{1}{4}$ in].

MACHINING SPECIAL FABRICS

A number of fabrics have special sewing requirements, particularly where needles are concerned.

Sheer fabrics like voile, organdie, batiste or chiffon look best with encased seams that don't detract from their delicate appearance. Remove selvedges [selvages] first to prevent puckering. The main problem lies with sheers being so thin and slippery to handle. Practice will help; take an offcut and run up a sample seam using the correct (new) needle and thread. The recommended needle size is 60–75 [8–11], with a fine cotton or polyester thread and a stitch length of 1.5–2 mm [approx $\frac{1}{16}$ in]. A single-hole needle plate can help to stabilize the fabric surface as the needle punches through. You can also try sewing with tissue paper under the fabric.

Denim looks tough enough in a finished garment but it frays easily and – like sheer fabrics – requires encased seams. Use a 75–90 [11–14] needle.

Velvets, due to the pile, can be as difficult as sheer fabrics and unpicking stitches from velvet leaves marks. Tacking [basting] should consist of short stitches with the occasional back stitch. On the machine, velvet takes a stitch length of 2–2.5 mm [approx $\frac{1}{16}$ in] with a loosened thread tension, using a 75–90 [11–14]

needle. Once again, practise on offcuts. If the velvet layers shift about, tack [baste] *and* pin firmly in the seam allowance before you begin. As you stitch, hold the bottom layer taut without dragging on the needle. Remove the pins as you go.

Knits must be handled with care while machining, as it is all too easy to stretch them out of shape. Work at a gentle speed and remember that your seams need to give a little with the natural stretch of jersey fabric. Change your regular needle to a 75–90 [11–14] ballpoint that won't split the fibres as it sews. Use the stretch stitch on your machine, if you have it, or the tricot. Otherwise, try zigzag on the narrowest setting. Knits do not unravel so seam finishing is not necessary. However, you may feel that certain seams – shoulders and waists, for example – could benefit from being taped (p. 30).

Stretching seam

Seam stretched in wear

MACHINING AN ENCASED SEAM

The sequence for machining a French seam is the same as it is for hand sewing (p. 25).

The flat fell seam

Sometimes called 'run and fell', this is another type of encased seam, widely used for tough-wearing casual clothes, skirts, trousers [pants], jeans and fabric bags. It is completely reversible with two visible rows of stitching on each side.

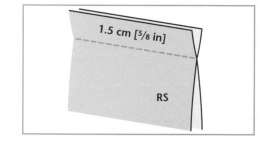

1 Pin wrong sides together and stitch with a 1.5 cm (⁵/₈ in) seam allowance.

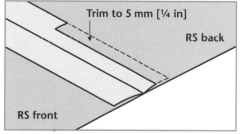

2 Press open and trim one side of the allowance to 5 mm (¼ in).

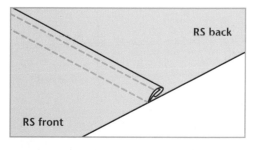

3 Fold uncut seam allowance in half, press and fold over to enclose previously cut edge. Pin, tack [baste] and machine along fold.

MACHINED SEAM FINISHES

The sequence for machining a bias binding is the same as it is for hand sewing (p. 30), except that the final slip stitch (Step 3) may be replaced by machine stitching too. Here are some other solutions to seam finishing.

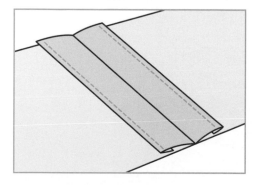

Edge stitched Stitch 3–6 mm [¹/₈–¼ in] from the raw edge on each side. Fold over on the stitch line and stitch close to the edge of the fold.

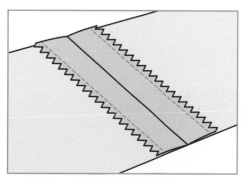

Stitched and pinked A finish for close-woven fabrics that prevents curling. Stitch to 6 mm [¼ in] from the edge of each seam allowance. Trim close to stitching with pinking shears.

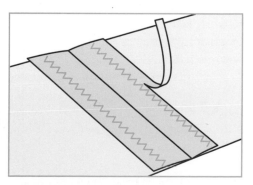

Zigzagged and trimmed Zigzag stitch down the edge of each allowance on the widest stitch setting but do not stitch over the edge. Trim close to stitching with shears.

MAKING DARTS

Darts give shape to flat fabric and enable it to fit over curved contours, for example on the bodice of a dress or the back of an armchair. They are marked by small dots on a paper pattern and are transferred to the fabric at the cutting-out stage with a fabric marker or tailor's chalk.

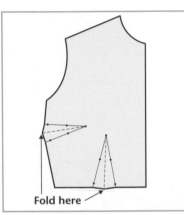

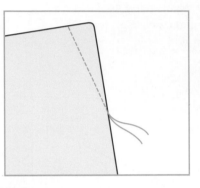

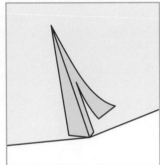

1 Match pattern dots together by folding down the centre. You will see that the stitch line will eventually form a triangle.

2 Pin, tack [baste] and machine the dart to a sharp point by stitching past the edge of the fabric. Raise presser foot and cut threads, leaving sufficient length to finish neatly by hand.

3 Darts in lightweight fabrics do not usually need trimming. Simply press the folded edge of the dart to one side without creasing the main fabric. Darts in thick fabric should be cut open on the fold and trimmed back before pressing.

SHAPED FACINGS

Facings are used to neaten the edges of necklines and armholes [armscyes] and are cut to the same shape and, most importantly, *on the same grain or bias* as the main garment. They can be stiffened a little with an interfacing if required, sewn or ironed on to the facing itself. It is easier to edge stitch or trim the outer edges of the facings with pinking shears before attaching.

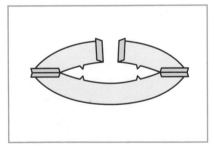

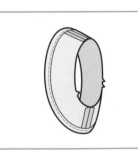

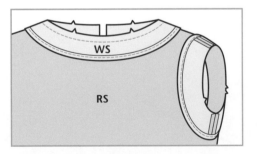

1 The facing for a neckline, showing the joins between front and back sections, and the ends turned back where they are to meet the fastening on the main piece.

2 The facing for an armhole [armscye] prepared with edge stitching.

3 The facings attached to the main garment, ready for the curved seams to be clipped (p. 25) and turned right sides out.

INSERTING A ZIP FASTENER

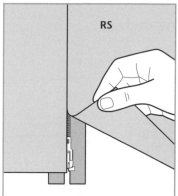

1 Set the zip [zipper] into the seam in the closed position. The fabric edges should meet at the centre and conceal the teeth.

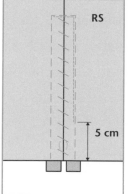

2 Cross-tack [baste] the zip [zipper] with the ends of the zip tape turned down. Tack [baste] around the stitch line as well, passing about 2.5 cm [1 in] clear of the end of the zip teeth. Start machining 5 cm [2 in] below the zip head in order to keep a straight line.

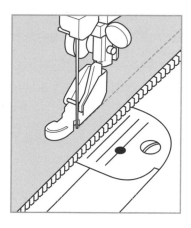

3 Topstitch around the zip [zipper] using the zipper foot to run close to the edge of the opening. Stop 5 cm [2 in] short of the zip head on the other side and, removing the cross-tacking [basting], slide the zip head down in order to complete the stitching at both sides of the top.

TOPSTITCHING

Topstitching can be used for purely decorative purposes and is frequently done in a contrasting colour around lapels and pockets. Use a longer stitch than you would for ordinary seam sewing.

MACHINING A BUTTONHOLE

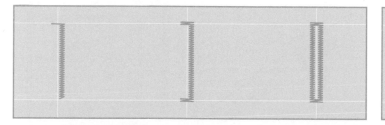

1 Mark the desired position of the buttonhole(s) with a fabric marker or tailor's chalk. Using a zigzag machine foot, set the stitch selector and make a few stitches to form the 'bar' of the buttonhole before travelling steadily down the first side. Make the second bar at the bottom and then turn the fabric through 180 degrees to complete the other side.

2 Pierce the centre of the buttonhole with embroidery scissors or a seam ripper and cut open carefully from end to end without clipping the bars.

SHIRRING

Shirring looks very like smocking without the embroidery. It is ideal for nightwear and beachwear. Shirring elastic is specially manufactured for use in sewing machines and is easier to apply than stitching down flat elastic. As with all techniques that you try for the first time, it is advisable to practise on an offcut before sewing your main piece.

1 Fill your bobbin by hand with shirring elastic and load it into your machine as usual. Adjust the thread tension to 4 and change from straight stitch to the longest, widest zigzag that your settings will allow.

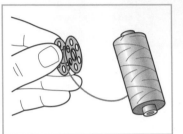

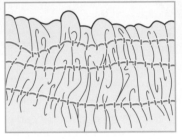

2 You will need to complete three or four rows before achieving the smocked effect. This shows the wrong side.

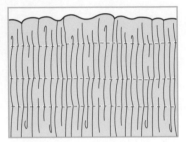

3 And this is the right side. Shirring works equally well on plain and patterned fabrics.

MAKING PIPING [CORDING]

Piping [cording] makes a smart external seam finish for clothes and home furnishings. The cord should be pre-shrunk; check when buying. It comes in various thicknesses, so use whatever is appropriate for your fabric. Piping needs to be supple and bend around corners so it is encased in bias-cut strips (p. 30).

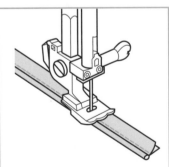

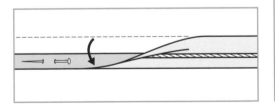

1 Pin the cord into the fabric and tack [baste], leaving a normal seam allowance.

2 Use a piping foot for best results, although a zipper foot performs well too. Stitch as close as possible to the cord. You can produce a continuous strip of piping to be cut up and used as required.

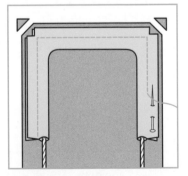

3 Alternatively, pin the piping in place and tack [baste] it to shape before machining. If turnings are bulky, layer them and cut off the excess to give neatly turned corners.

PROJECT: DACHSHUND DRAUGHT EXCLUDER

A faithful dog with floppy ears to guard you against draughts – and he can fit across any door simply by adjusting the length between his head and tail.

Any type of fabric is suitable, including knits. Make a paper pattern by ruling a large sheet of paper with a grid of 9 cm [3 ½ in] squares. Scale up the pieces, square by square, from the grid below. Cut out the paper templates and pin to the fabric, noting which pieces must go on a fold. *When cutting out the fabric add a 12 mm [½ in] seam allowance all round.*

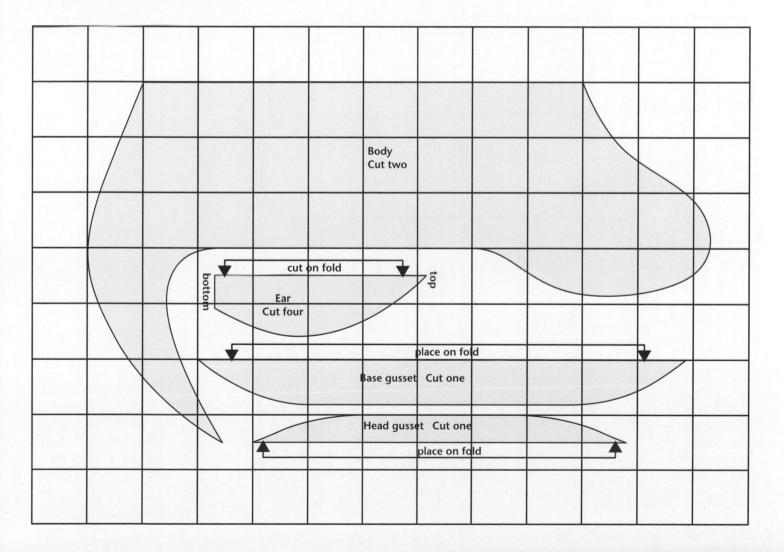

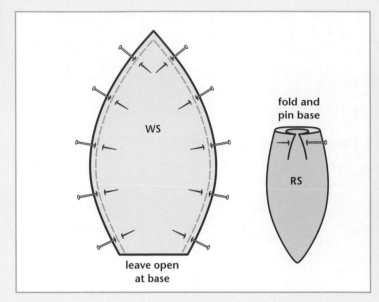

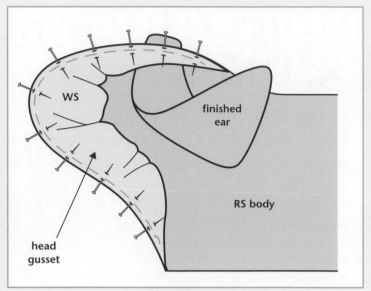

1 To make a pair of ears, pin each pair of shapes RS facing and stitch right round except for the base. Turn RS out. Fold, pin and tack [baste] a small pleat in each.

2 On the RS of one half of the main body, pin and firmly tack [baste] the head gusset as shown, stitching one of the finished ears between the two layers of fabric. Repeat with the other half of the body and the second ear.

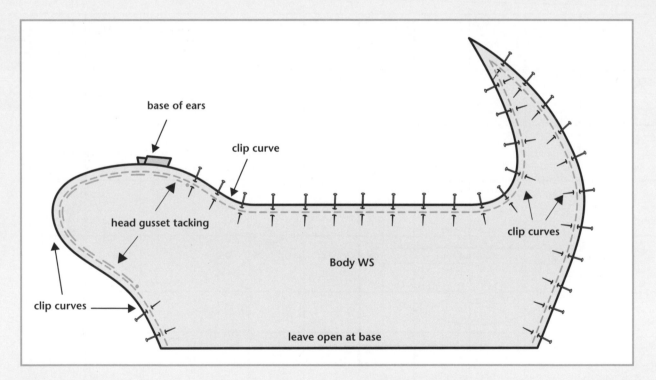

3 RS facing, with the ear flaps safely clear of the needle, machine stitch each half of the dog's head to its own side of the head gusset.

4 Machine stitch the remaining halves of the body together from chin to base, and from neck up to tip of tail and down the other side. Leave the base itself open. Clip curves in preparation for turning. Remove all tacking [basting].

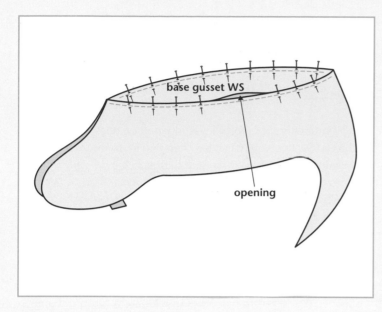

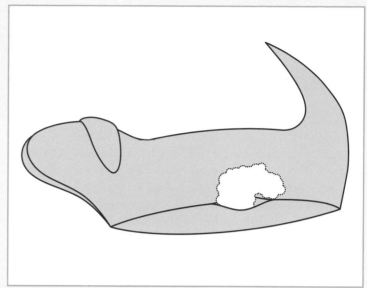

5 Still WS out, fit the base gusset as shown. Machine stitch around both sides of the body, leaving an opening of 10–12 cm [4–5 in] for stuffing.

6 Turn the dog RS out and use a knitting needle to push his tail to a fine point. Stuff the head and body as firmly as you can with polyester toy filling. You may need a good deal, depending on his length.

7 Close the raw edges of the opening and oversew.

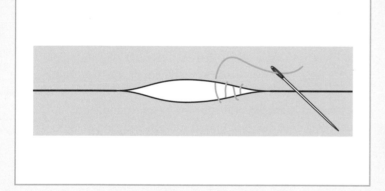

8 Use buttons, felt appliqué or embroidery for the dog's eyes, nose and mouth, giving him a unique personality. Fix a collar or bow around his neck as a finishing touch.

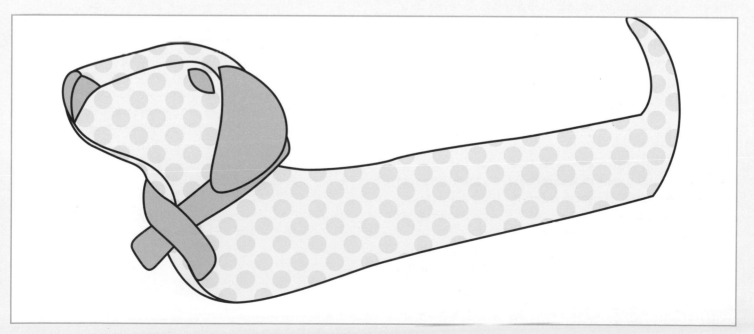

LAUNDRY & AFTERCARE

Laundering

Always look for the care symbols on any fabric that you buy; the manufacturer's care label appears on the bolt itself and you should also ask the shop assistant for a care ticket to take away with your purchase. This is useful to keep as part of a record of everything that you make. Other points of reference are your own washing machine and tumble dryer manuals. These contain details of all the washing and drying programs, indicating how they tie in with the standard care symbols.

If possible, deal quickly with stains. Don't rub the affected area too hard because friction can damage the fibres and leave an obvious patch. Oil-based marks should be tackled from the wrong side of the fabric with a proper solvent; follow the manufacturer's instructions.

Whether washing by hand or machine, do not use washing powder on fabrics with a high wool or silk content. Instead, choose soap flakes or a liquid for delicate fabrics. The cleansing agents in liquid soaps are designed to work at low temperatures and won't leave a powdery deposit. Test strong colours (especially reds) for colourfastness and if in any doubt wash them separately. Woollen or wool-mix fabrics of any kind should always be rinsed in warm water. Use the machine-washable wool setting on your machine, not the low-temperature or hand-wash program that delivers a cold rinse.

Tumble dryers are large contributors to accidental shrinkage, and some fabrics are better left to dry without heat. Lift woollens from the washing machine and roll in a clean towel to remove excess water. Lay any knit fabrics, including jersey, to dry flat on a drying rack. Do not peg them up because they could lose shape as the moisture drains downward.

Iron fabrics according to the recommended heat setting. Take extra care if you have added trimmings. Nylon lace, metallic threads and plastic sequins will shrivel at the touch of a hot iron.

'Pressing' is often used for 'ironing' but more strictly it means using steam and a pressing cloth. It is important to lift the iron straight up and down and avoid pulling it across the fabric when steam pressing. Make use of your sleeveboard, roll or tailor's ham (p. 10) to smooth awkward surfaces and contours.

Aftercare

After all your effort, it's worth investing in good quality hangers for the clothes that you make. Sew hanging loops inside shoulder seams and waistbands to make sure garments are properly supported, not drooping in deep folds from a distorted shoulder line. Evening dresses and other delicate fabrics should hang inside protective covers to keep them clear of the floor and free from too much handling.

When placing clothes and household linen in storage, the golden rule is always to put items away clean, absolutely dry, and unstarched (the silverfish pest loves to eat starch). Dust, dirt and perspiration can harm and discolour fibres of all kinds – synthetics as well as natural – and both moths and moulds feed readily on dirt.

Precious heirlooms like christening and wedding gowns should be laundered or dry cleaned, then interleaved with plenty of acid-free tissue paper and stored in zipped cotton cases. Keep curtains, loose covers and bed quilts folded neatly and well-protected in chests and cupboards, or inside zipped covers and lidded plastic boxes for long-term storage. Shake them out occasionally and refold a different way – this will prevent permanent creases from setting in.

Avoid the risk of mould or mildew by never storing fabrics in poorly ventilated, damp or humid surroundings such as lofts, cellars or seldom-opened cupboards. Low-powered heaters and dehumidifiers can help to reduce problems caused by damp and condensation.

Stay vigilant for the tiny clothes moth. It has a life cycle of around six weeks, and it is the larvae that make ruinous holes in things. Nowadays, there are pleasantly scented alternatives to camphor mothballs, such as cedarwood blocks and lavender bags, although these need renewing from time to time. Moths not only lay their eggs on woollen fibres but can also damage silk, fur or feathers. It is a wise precaution to check your storage places every so often; keep disturbing the moths' potential habitat and they won't settle.

SEWING TERMS

Armscye (US) The armhole of a garment

Appliqué The technique of stitching one fabric on top of another

Basting (Tacking) Temporary stitches made with running stitch about 1.5 cm [1/2 in] long

Bias Any diagonal line between lengthwise and crosswise grains. 'True' bias, at 45 degrees to the selvedge [selvage], gives maximum stretch

Bias binding Binding strip cut on the bias to fit smoothly around curves without adding bulk. Purchase readymade, or cut from the fabric in hand to make a 'self' bias binding

Binding A narrow strip of fabric or tape used to cover the raw edges of a garment. It can be hidden on the inside or sewn on the surface as decoration

Blind hemming Hem stitches that attach a folded edge virtually invisibly to a flat surface

Calico Closely woven cotton fabric in a natural cream colour. (Americans often give the same name to printed cotton fabrics)

Casing A tube designed to contain elastic, cord, ribbon etc

Dart A sewn structure that takes in fabric to give shape to a garment

Ease The adjustable difference between body measurement and paper pattern, especially used for setting sleeves in an armhole [armscye]

Facing Shaped piece of fabric (frequently interfaced) enclosing raw edges inside a sleeve or neck opening

Fusible web A synthetic material that bonds to fabric when melted by the heat of an iron

Gathers Small folds gathered by drawing up a line of stitching. Used to create frills [ruffles]

Grain line The direction in which the warp and weft threads lie. The warp running lengthwise, parallel to the selvedge [selvage], is the lengthwise grain. The weft follows the crosswise grain, at right angles to the selvedge [selvage]

Hem The turned-up area at the bottom of a garment, which prevents fraying

Interfacing Extra fabric sewn or ironed between the layers of fabric to give it more body

Lining A lightweight fabric (often taffeta or satin) sewn inside a garment to conceal seam allowances. Linings also block 'see-through' in a lightweight fabric

Loom state As the fabric comes off the loom, before it has undergone any further process. Loom state cloth will shrink

Muslin A translucent loose-woven cotton fabric

Nap Texture or design that runs in one direction only and influences pattern cutting layouts. 'With nap' fabrics include velvet, corduroy and satin

Notches Diamond-shaped marks that project beyond the pattern edge, for aligning pattern pieces at the sewing stage

Notions Incidental items such as thread, fastenings, tape and trimmings

Petersham Corded ribbon (similar to grosgrain) used to stiffen waistbands and also in millinery

Pile The soft raised surface on velvet, corduroy and some brushed fabrics. It usually has a nap that can affect the colour and influences pattern cutting layouts

Piping [cording] Gives a neat firm finish to a seam, especially on soft furnishings. The cord should be pre-shrunk and encased in bias-cut strips

Pleat Folds controlling fabric fullness. Variations include box, inverted and knife pleats

Poppers [Snaps] Press stud fastenings

Pre-shrunk Fabric subjected to a shrinking process during manufacture

Pressing Often used for 'ironing' but more strictly means using steam and a pressing cloth

RS Abbreviation for 'Right Side'

Raw edge Untreated cut edge of a piece of fabric, which may fray or unravel

Rise Distance from crotch seam to waistband on trousers [pants]

Rouleau Narrow tubing constructed from bias strips, used for shoulder straps and applied decoration

Seam Two pieces of fabric joined with a line of stitches. Variations include open, encased, French and flat fell seams

Seam allowance Distance between the cut edge and the seam line

Selvedge [Selvage] The solid edge of a woven fabric

Slip stitch Stitches that attach a folded edge virtually invisibly to a flat surface

Snaps (Poppers) Press stud fastenings

Stay stitching A line of straight stitches that prevents curved or bias edges, such as necklines, shoulders and waistlines, from stretching out of shape during sewing

Tacking [Basting] Temporary stitches made with running stitch about 1.5 cm [1/2 in] long

Tailor's tacks Temporary loops of thread for matching points or marking the position of darts or pockets

Topstitching An extra row of stitching (usually decorative) done in matching or contrasting thread along or near a finished edge

WS Abbreviation for 'Wrong Side'

Warp Runs lengthwise, parallel to the selvedge [selvage], usually stronger than the weft

Weft Runs at right angles to the selvedge [selvage], not usually quite as strong as the warp

PATCHWORK

Patchwork is a craft for people of all ages. There is such a variety of shapes and designs to choose from that everyone should find something to suit their tastes and capabilities. This section has been prepared with the beginner in mind, taking them through the methods and techniques in easy stages. However, it also features plenty of templates and patterns to inspire more experienced stitchers to try their hands, perhaps at a dazzling Mennonite star or delicate Hawaiian appliqué.

You don't have to make an entire quilt all at once. Piece together just one intricate block of patchwork and if you go no further, you have a unique cushion cover or a decorative panel for the side of a tote bag. Using scraps, young children can start on a simple cover for a doll's bed or cheerful padded pan holders; the basic four- or nine-piece block makes an easy introduction for them. The terminology used is UK-standard, together with the relevant US terms in square brackets [ ] to make this a practical guide for all readers.

Although strongly associated now with North America, it was the ingenuity of European immigrants that laid the foundations of patchwork, quilting and appliqué there. As the incomers arrived and spread westwards, their expertise and patterns travelled along with them. The same diamond-pieced pattern named *Ship's Wheel* in Massachusetts became *Harvest Sun* in the Midwest where there was no ocean but acre upon acre of cornfields. The most famous pattern of all, *Log Cabin,* says everything about the pioneering lifestyle of the early settlers.

Making the most of scarce resources, warm bed covers were cleverly pieced and quilted in styles that were regularly handed down to younger generations of women by their mothers and grandmothers. The bridal quilt represented the peak of a young woman's stitching skills, after she had spent so much of her girlhood perfecting them.

As people grew more affluent, they bought manufactured items rather than making them at home. But this meant they could also buy brand new fabrics in larger quantities, and so quiltmaking – including hand stitching and appliqué – developed as a decorative art and spread back to Europe once again. The traditional designs with evocative names like *Birds in the Air*, *Prairie Queen* and *Drunkard's Path* have been preserved to this day and continue to be worked expertly by enthusiastic quilters all over the world.

PART ONE:
EQUIPMENT AND MATERIALS

TEMPLATES

Templates are used for cutting out multiple pattern pieces.

Made from metal, plastic or card, templates may be bought readymade from needlecraft suppliers, or cut out carefully at home from graph paper stuck on to strong card or acetate. There are three types (arrows indicate fabric grain direction, see p.14):

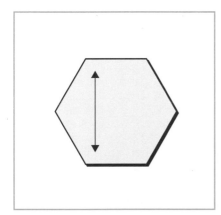

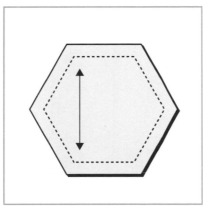

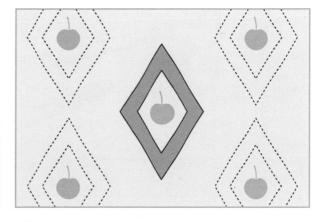

1 Exact size and shape of the finished patch – use when cutting papers for hand sewing (p. 68). No seam allowance, cut fabric with 6 mm [¼ in] extra all round.

2 Incorporates the shape *and* a 6 mm [¼ in] seam allowance – use when cutting fabric for machine sewing.

3 Inner margin marks the actual patch size; outer margin adds seam allowance. Window helps to centre a motif.

EQUIPMENT

A **Sharps needles** for general sewing with standard cotton or polyester thread; **betweens** for fine stitching and quilting.

B Coloured glass- or plastic-headed **pins** are easier to see and handle.

C Medium thickness (No 50) cotton **thread** for hand sewing patchwork. A stronger cotton (No 40) or cotton/polyester mix should be used for machine sewing. Thread up with the free end straight off the reel [spool] and not only will it pass more easily through the needle's eye, it won't tangle while you work.

D To hand sew more quickly and smoothly, draw your thread across a block of **beeswax**. Wax treatment combats high humidity and kills static electricity from synthetics.

E A **thimble** is necessary for pushing needles through several layers of fabric at once. Some quilters wear one on each hand.

F A **seam ripper** for removing machine stitching. Use with care as it is all too easy to pierce surrounding fabric.

G **Dressmaking shears** have asymmetric handles and long blades for cutting smoothly through fabric at a low angle on a flat surface. Do not allow anyone – including yourself – to blunt [dull] them by cutting paper, card, string or sticky tape.

H **Embroidery scissors** for precision cutting. The blades are 3–10 cm [1.25–4 in] in length and sharply pointed.

I **Craft knife** for cutting templates. Use in conjunction with a self-healing cutting mat (**J**) and metal straight edge (**K**). Change blades frequently.

L A **rotary cutter** rapidly cuts strips and several layers of fabric at once. Change blades frequently. A locking mechanism retracts the blade for safety. Use in conjunction with a cutting mat (**J**) and rotary ruler that has straight and diagonal markings (see p. 66).

M **Acrylic dressmaker's ruler** marked with a grid to help you draw accurate templates.

N **Ruler** marked in cms and inches.

O **Gauge** fitted with a sliding marker that allows you to set it on a fixed measurement.

P **Pair of compasses** for drawing curved templates.

Q **Protractor** for measuring angles of templates.

R **Quilter's fabric-marking pencil**

S **Dressmaker's chalk pencil with brush end**

T **Graph paper** for drawing accurate templates and drafting patterns.

U **Spray adhesive** for sticking paper templates to card.

V **Glue stick** for temporarily positioning appliqué shapes. Test on scrap fabric first.

W **Sewing machine**

X **Iron**

FABRIC

Use fabrics of similar weights for best results and pre-wash to guard against shrinkage and colour runs. Refer to p. 14 for details on weave, grain and bias.

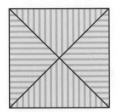 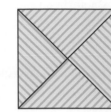 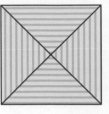

Texture comes from the weave of a fabric. It also depends whether the cloth has a distinct 'nap' or 'pile', like velvet or corduroy (see left), which can be brushed in different directions. You can show ingenuity with texture, even when the patches are identical.

Pattern-making is limitless with patchwork. Try the templates in various combinations. Striped and checked fabrics can be used most effectively, and you can play around with the scale of prints too.

The colour circle provides a lesson in colour harmonies. Red, yellow and blue are the primary colours. The secondary colours are green, orange and purple from mixtures of the primaries. The tertiary colours lie between the primaries and secondaries. Colours directly opposite each other on the circle are complementary and make the most vibrant combinations. Those next to each other are called analogous. Colours from red to yellow-green occupy the 'warm' spectrum, while from green to red-purple they are described as 'cool'.

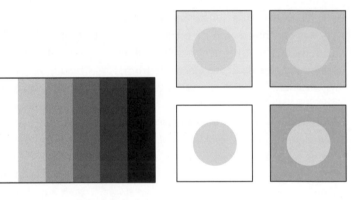

1 Colour 'value' refers to the relative lightness or darkness of a colour.

2 These values are significantly affected by adjoining colours.

Wadding [batting] and lining or backing

Wadding [batting] is the soft fibrous material sandwiched for warmth between the top of a quilt and the lining fabric. It may be totally synthetic, like polyester, or consist of natural fibre, such as wool or cotton, mixed with polyester. Lining – with or without wadding [batting] – neatens and strengthens a quilt. Pre-shrunk dress-weight cotton is ideal.

Shrinkage

The tighter the weave, the less likely a fabric is to shrink during or after manufacture. The shop label should say if a fabric is pre-shrunk. *If it is not, you must do it yourself before cutting out.* Immerse in plain hot water for half an hour. This also reveals any problems with colour fastness.

Fat quarters

A fat quarter means getting larger pieces of fabric than possible from a standard quarter of a yard, including strips twice as long on the lengthwise grain. The metric system in Europe does not cater for fat quarters at most retailers, but they are readily available online.

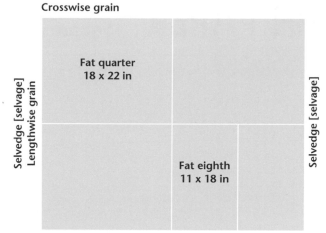

Crosswise grain

Selvedge [selvage] Lengthwise grain

Fat quarter
18 x 22 in

Fat eighth
11 x 18 in

Selvedge [selvage]

One yard of fabric, 36 x 44 in

Regular quarter yard, 9 x 44 in

Calculating quantities

The standard widths for fabric are 90, 115 and 150 cm [36, 44–45 and 54 in]. Dress-weight fabric is usually 115 cm [44–45 in]; muslin and interfacings come in 90 cm [36 in] widths.

Study your pattern. How many different templates does it use? How many patches of each shape? Before calculating, take 5 cm [2 in] off the width for shrinkage and removal of selvedges [selvages]. *Be sure to include seam allowances.*

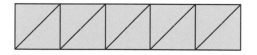

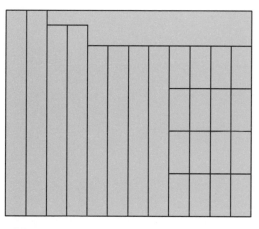

1 See how many times a template fits into the fabric width and divide that number into the total number of patches required of that particular shape.

2 Do the same for the number of lengthwise strips for borders and sashing (p. 76–7).

3 For linings, be prepared to piece together two or three widths, depending on the quilt size.

To estimate the length of fabric needed after 1 and 2, divide the total number of patches by the number in a single width and multiply the result by the width of the template.

An economical cutting plan takes straight strips from one edge of the fabric and irregular shapes from the other. Bias-binding or piping around the edges uses strips cut on the diagonal, which will lead to some wastage.

GRAPH PAPER **Square grid**

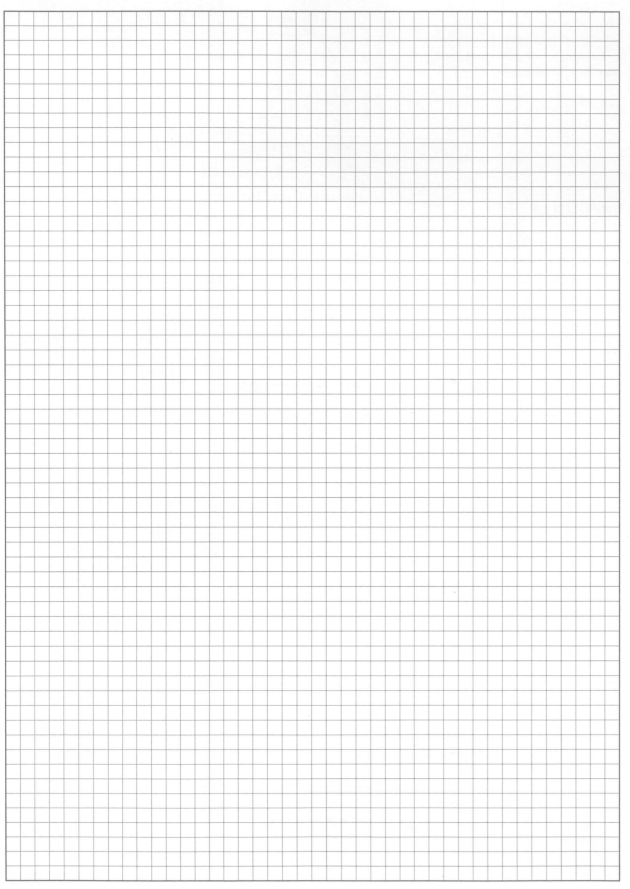

GRAPH PAPER Isometric

CURVED TEMPLATES

Shell

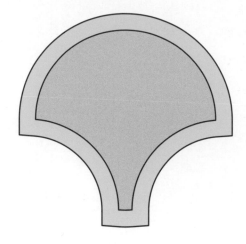

Drunkard's path

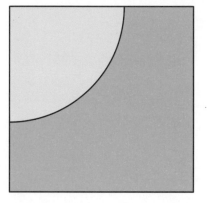

Double axehead

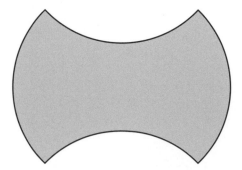

PART TWO:
PIECED PATCHWORK METHODS AND TECHNIQUES

Before undertaking a full-sized quilt or wall hanging, try something smaller for your first attempt at patchwork. Table toppers, place mats, cushion covers and cot quilts are all good starter projects.

GRAPHS

Choose a design in scale with the finished piece. A big repeat pattern is clearly not suitable for a baby's quilt but at the same time, don't make something with scores of tiny patches that takes too long to finish.

Graph paper, squared (pp. 60 and 99) and isometric (p. 61), will serve for drafting out your overall pattern, and then for drawing individual patches to the precise shape and size you require. Decide which of the three types of template you need (p. 55) depending on whether you are cutting papers, hand or machine sewing.

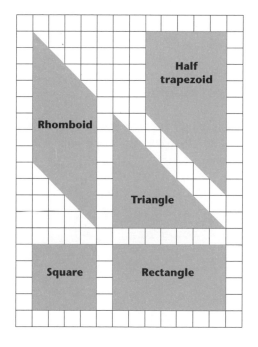

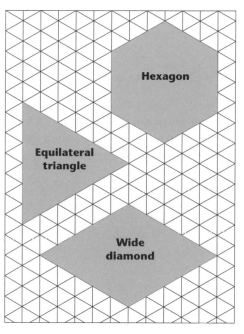

MAKING TEMPLATES

Cut out the shapes carefully from the graph paper because these will form your templates. The slightest inaccuracy now becomes a bigger problem at the sewing stage.

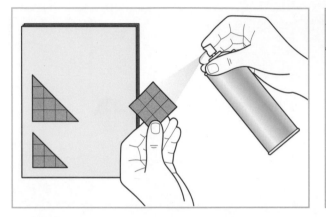

1 With spray adhesive, glue each shape to a sheet of mounting board or acetate.

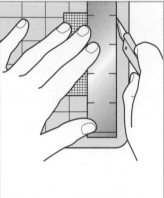

2 Cut out the templates with a sharp craft knife and metal straight edge. Keep fingers clear of the blade.

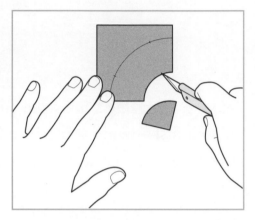

3 Cut notches into any curved templates. Notches are later marked on the fabric to help match pieces when joining.

Label the templates with an arrow for grain direction (p. 55) and 'This way up' if there is any risk of confusion. Also, make a note on them of how many of each shape you need, and from which fabric. Detailed preparation saves time.

Medium-grade sandpaper can be used for templates. It is perfect for short-term projects and grips the fabric well when marking out. A whole sheet of sandpaper placed under slippery fabric holds it steady while tracing.

STANDARD SHAPES

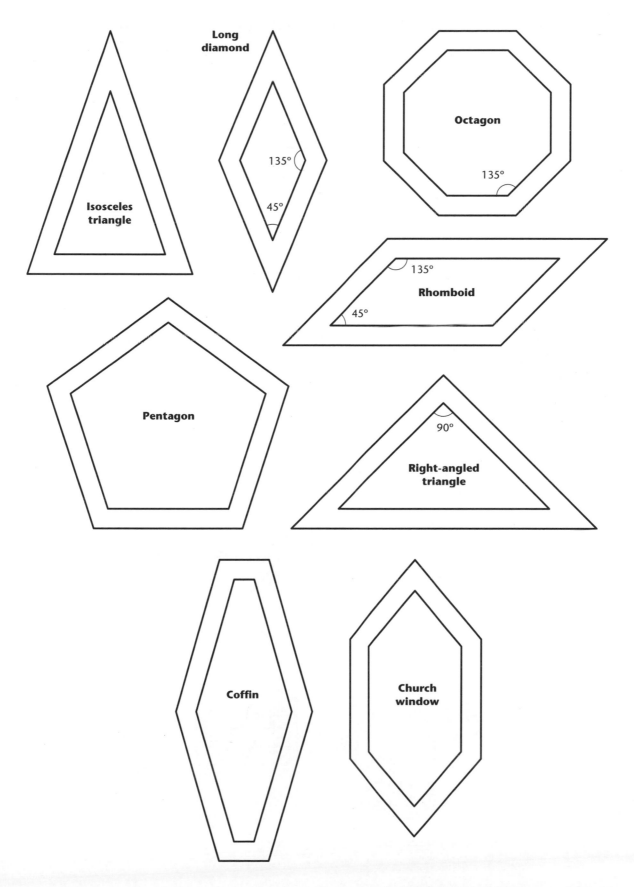

Isosceles triangle

Long diamond
135°
45°

Octagon
135°

Rhomboid
135°
45°

Pentagon

Right-angled triangle
90°

Coffin

Church window

CUTTING SHAPES FROM FABRIC

With a sharp pencil, mark patchwork shapes on the wrong side (WS) of your fabric, starting with any border strips or sashing (pp. 76–7). Cut long pieces with the grain and curved ones on the bias.

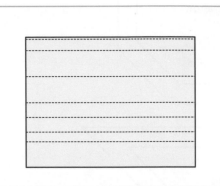

1 Include a 6 mm [¼ in] seam allowance on strips. For accuracy, use a straight edge squared up with a dressmaker's ruler.

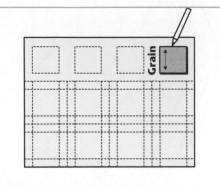

2 Templates for hand sewing are marked out with a 6 mm [¼ in] margin. With practice, you can do this by eye.

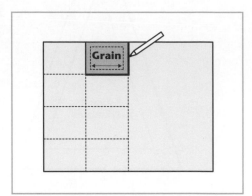

3 Templates for machine sewing include seam allowances and need no margins. However, accurate cutting is essential.

Using a rotary cutter and ruler

Remember to include a 6 mm [¼ in] seam allowance. Spray-starch and press the main strips before cutting further.

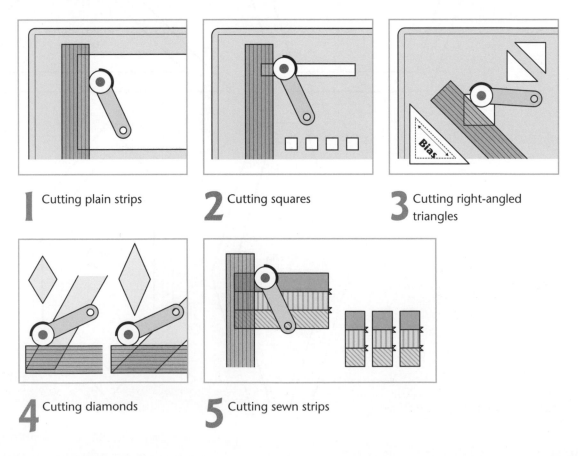

1 Cutting plain strips

2 Cutting squares

3 Cutting right-angled triangles

4 Cutting diamonds

5 Cutting sewn strips

SEMINOLE PATCHWORK

Strip-pieced Seminole – often used for decorative borders – is named after the American Indians of Southern Florida, whose vibrant machine-sewn patchwork developed around 1920.

Use pre-shrunk, solid-colour fabric for Seminole. Remove the selvedges [selvages] and cut into strips; lightly spray-starch and press. After sewing, press seams to one side, preferably towards darker fabrics to prevent show-through. Cut into more strips.

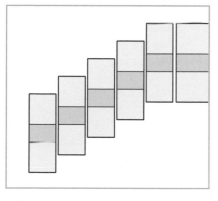

1 Arrange pieced strips into the desired pattern.

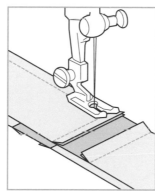

2 Sew strips together, first in pairs; then continue piecing until the band is completed.

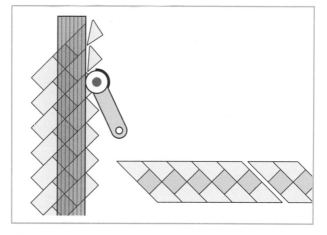

3 Trim top and bottom edges with 6 mm [¼ in] seam allowance.

Border designs

Bold, clear colours give the best results. Three or four colours make a simple pattern look really intricate.

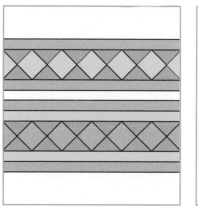

1 Sew one or more straight-grain edging strips to the main band for different effects.

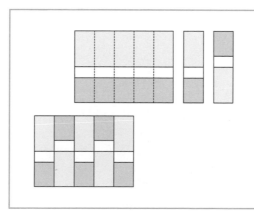

2 Sew three colours together in varying widths. Cut, and reverse alternate strips.

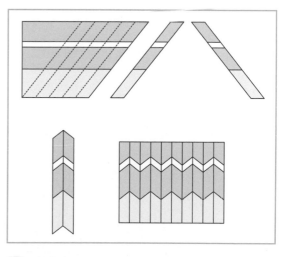

3 Make a zigzag pattern with strips cut at an angle of 45 degrees. Take care not to stretch when sewing.

ENGLISH PATCHWORK

One-shape hexagon patchwork is traditionally associated with English hand-sewn designs, made from cotton fabric folded neatly over backing papers.

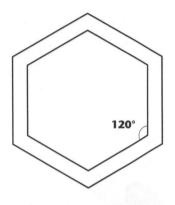

120°

The inner hexagon of this window gives the finished patch size and is also a template for the papers (p. 55); cut them from old magazine or catalogue pages. Use the outer margin of the window template for cutting out the patch plus seam allowance. Alternatively, pin a paper to the fabric first and cut round it with 6 mm [¼ in] allowance.

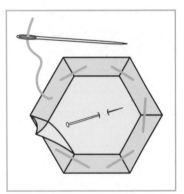

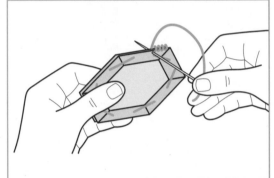

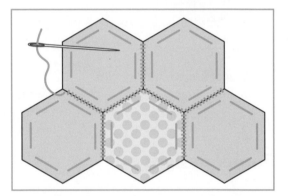

1 Pin paper to fabric. Folding fabric over as you go, tack [baste] through fabric and paper, right around the patch. This holds everything in place until final stitching is done. Prepare all hexagons this way.

2 Join patches by placing RS together and oversew one side neatly from corner to corner. Keep stitches small, just catching the fold of fabric each time.

3 Make a single rosette by joining six hexagons around a central one. Double and treble rosettes are formed by adding further rings of patches. Do not break off your thread but go as far as you can with one length. Tacking [basting] and papers stay in position until the final stages of a project.

Hand-sewing stitches for patchwork

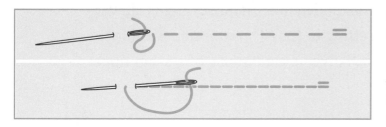

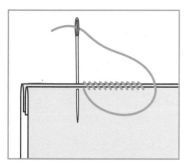

Running stitch (left) Secure thread with two small stitches. Push needle in and out of fabric evenly.

Back stitch (lower left) Start as for running stitch but go back over the first space. Needle out again at one stitch length ahead of last stitch made. Repeat, with needle back in at the point where previous stitch ends.

Oversewing or **whip stitch** Secure thread with two small stitches on the spot and proceed with neat diagonal stitches equally spaced. Sew from left to right or vice versa.

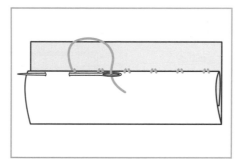

Slip stitch attaches a folded edge invisibly to a flat surface. Take up a few threads of flat fabric with your needle, enter fold and slide along inside before emerging to make the next stitch.

PROJECT: PLACE MAT

The mat features a single rosette stitched to plain foundation fabric. From the foundation fabric, cut two hexagons to the desired size of the mat, plus 1 cm [³/₈ in] seam allowance. A third layer of non-woven interfacing is optional.

Calculate the rosette size and, from that, the size of a single hexagon. Follow the instructions for making a template (p. 64). Cut papers with the template and sew the rosette as shown opposite. Remove the tacking [basting] and papers and press face down.

Pin and tack [baste] the rosette to the RS of one of the large hexagons. Attach it by slip stitching to the foundation fabric. Topstitch neatly round each hexagon for extra firmness. Use perle [pearl] embroidery thread for a decorative effect.

Pin and tack [baste] the two large hexagons RS together. Machine around five sides without sewing through the rosette. Clip corners, turn the mat RS out and slip stitch the remaining side closed. Press face down.

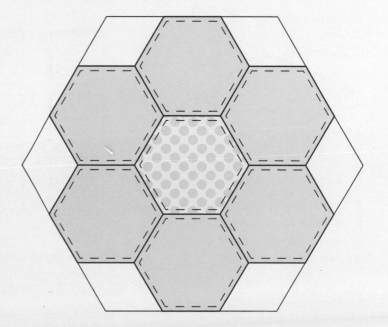

TO SEW BY HAND OR MACHINE?

Both methods are acceptable – it's a matter of personal preference. Hand sewing is slower but some processes, like folding sharp corners and setting in (p. 74), are easier. Machine sewing is quicker, and often stronger, but mistakes will involve careful use of a seam ripper.

Hand sewing without papers

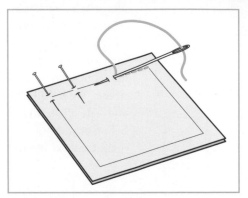

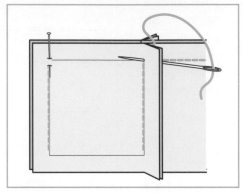

1 Pin patches RS together, matching the marked lines front and back. Sew small, even running stitches along the lines, starting and ending with a back stitch. Join several patches like this to form a row.

2 Join rows with running stitch. At each cross seam, do a back stitch as in 1. Needle through the seam allowance and make another back stitch. This ensures a neat join at each corner.

3 Press seams to one side, either towards darker fabrics to prevent show-through or to alternate sides to avoid bulk.

Piecing by machine

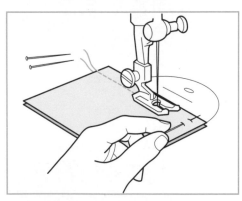

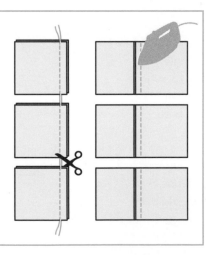

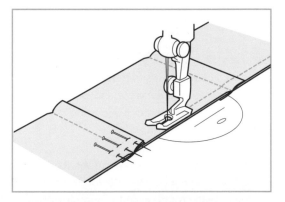

1 Pin patches RS together. In the absence of marked lines, stitch to a seam allowance set by the edge of the presser foot. Remove pins as you go.

2 Chain paired patches together to save time and thread. Cut apart and press seams to one side.

3 When joining rows, pin seam allowances in different directions to avoid bulk. Remove pins as you go.

JOINING TECHNIQUES

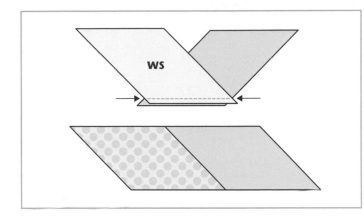

Offset seams Oblique-angled shapes such as rhomboids and diamonds should be offset when stitched together. When turned RS, they appear flush at the edges.

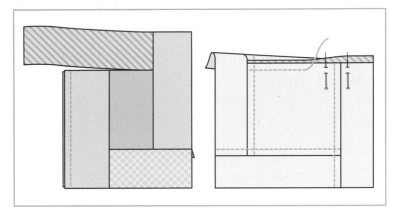

Joining right-angles To add the fourth strip around a central square: stitch halfway; open and pin the extended pieces to the new strip; complete the seam.

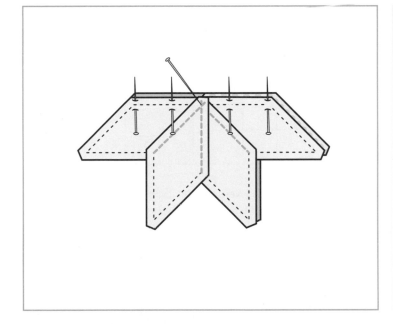

Eight-seam join To join two halves of an 8-point star: pin through the centre of both halves where the stitching meets at a point. Pin the rest of the two halves together along the seam allowance and hand-stitch with care so points meet accurately at the centre. Open flat and press all seams in one direction, twirling the centre as for set-ins (p. 75).

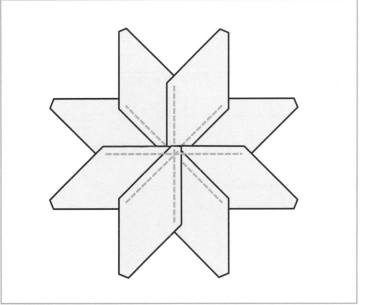

By machine Stitch the two halves together along the seam allowance, passing straight across the point of the topmost diamond. Open flat and press seams as they lie from the initial piecing.

BLOCKS

The block method of quilt construction is essentially American. Developed from early colonial days when the whole family slept under one huge quilt, manageable units were sewn separately and later assembled into an overall pattern.

Blocks are usually based on a grid; four-, five-, seven or nine-patch types are among the most common. Their distinctive regional names commemorate people, places and events of the times.

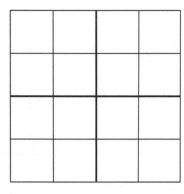 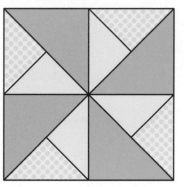

Whirligig The number of pieces in any four-patch block is always divisible by four.

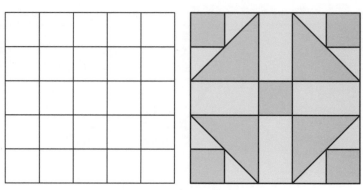

Grandmother's Choice Five-patch blocks are constructed on a grid of twenty-five squares.

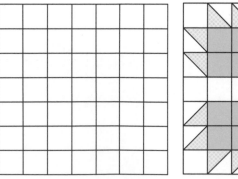 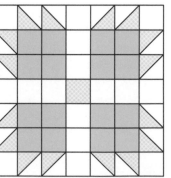

Bear's Tracks Less common, seven-patch blocks are based on forty-nine squares.

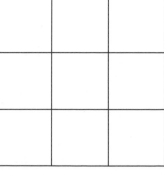 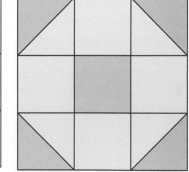

Snowball variation Nine-patch blocks are ideal for beginners and underlie many traditional patterns.

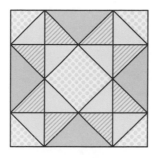

Full Moon (4-patch)

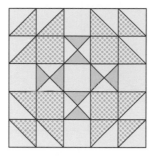

Tippecanoe (4-patch)

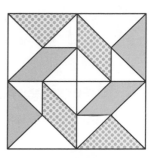

Windblown Square (4-patch)

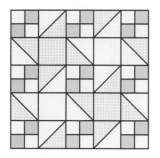

Milky Way (5-patch)

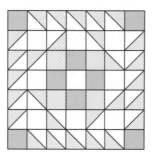

Handy Andy (5-patch)

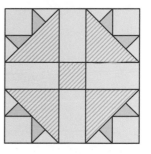

Cross and Crown (5-patch)

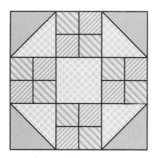

Lincoln's Platform (7-patch)

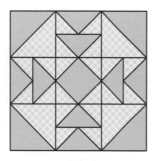

Prickly Pear (7-patch)

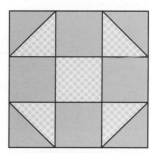

Country Roads (7-patch)

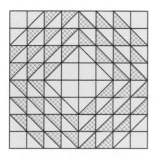

Prairie Queen (9-patch)

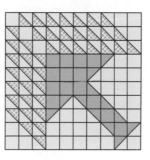

T-Block (9-patch)

Churn Dash (9-patch)

Ocean Wave (4-patch)

Pine Tree (5-patch)

Shoo-fly (9-patch)

SETTING IN

Hand setting in

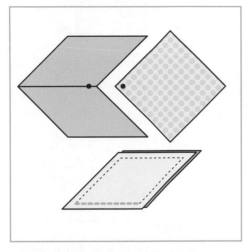

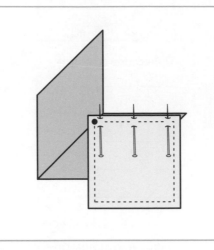

1 'Setting in' fits one piece into an angle formed by two others already joined. The seam on the first pair should end in a back stitch 6 mm (¼ in) from the edge.

2 RS together, pin the new piece into the angle with corners matching (see dots). Stitch from the outer edge into the corner, do a back stitch but do not cut thread.

3 Pull new piece round to pin its adjacent side into the angle. Stitch from the back stitch to the outer edge of the join.

Machine setting in

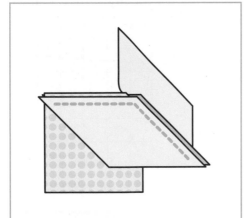

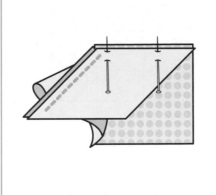

Where possible, avoid setting in at right-angles by piecing a block in horizontal or vertical strips that can be joined with straight seams.

1 RS together, pin the new piece into the angle with corners matching. Machine stitch from the corner to the outer edge. Cut thread.

2 Pull new piece round to pin its adjacent side into the angle. Stitch from the corner to the outer edge of the join.

Sewing curved seams

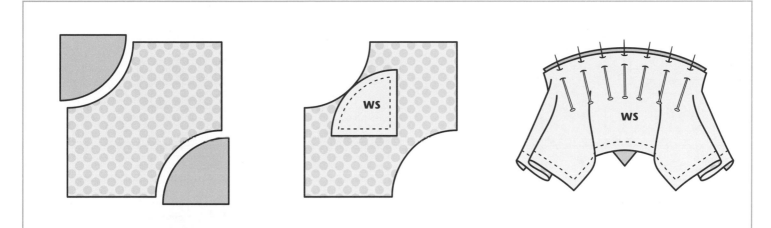

1 Match notches (p. 64) on both pieces and pin RS together from the centre outwards, easing the fit as you go.

Pressing hand and machine stitching

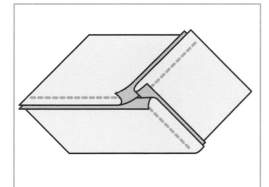

Hand-sewn set-ins should be twirled open before pressing to avoid bulk at the join. Press carefully on both sides.

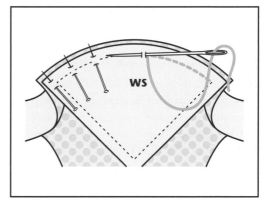

2 Starting and finishing with a back stitch, sew by hand or slowly by machine. Remove pins as you go.

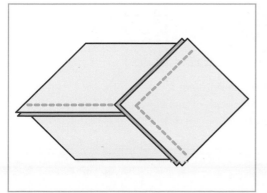

Machine-sewn set-in pieces are pressed towards the seam of the first pair, which is folded to one side. Press carefully on both sides.

PUTTING BLOCKS TOGETHER

These sets demonstrate four principal ways of putting quilt blocks together.

Edge to edge Blocks are joined directly to one another, often forming an intricate geometric pattern. A variation is to alternate pieced and plain blocks, increasing the patchwork area with no extra piecing.

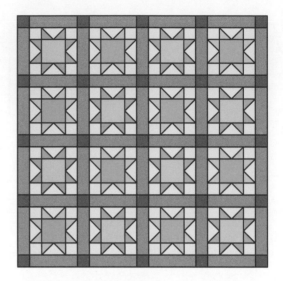

Sashing Also called 'latticing', where blocks are separated by narrow strips. Sashing may also be done in one direction only.

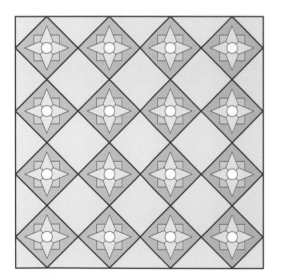

Diagonal Blocks are turned through 45 degrees and set on their points.

Strip Strips of alternating designs are sewn together; they may consist both of pieced work and plain or patterned fabric.

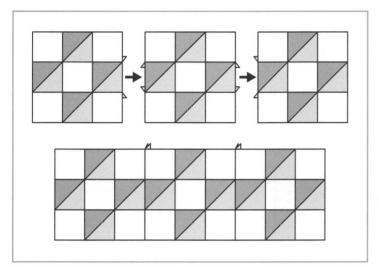

Joining edge to edge Blocks are joined to one another in rows. Each block is sewn, RS facing, to its neighbour with the normal 6 mm [¼ in] seam allowance. The allowances are pressed in different directions on adjacent rows.

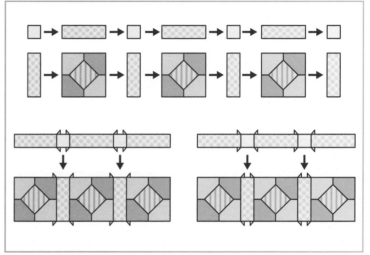

Joining sashing This particular style uses contrasting squares ('posts') at the intersections, so the sashing itself is pieced like a block. Seam allowances are pressed in opposite directions to avoid bulk.

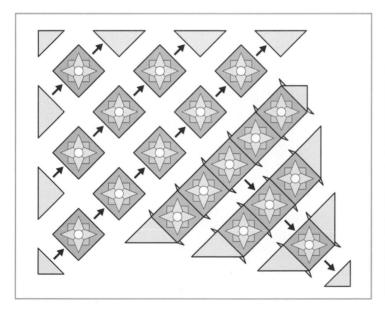

Joining diagonals The diagonal rows are squared off at the edges with half- and quarter-square pieces.

Stringing produces a totally new fabric from which other shapes and patterns may be created. It evolved from sewing narrow offcuts together at random. Nowadays it is often used for a planned effect. Creative cutting and re-piecing can give kaleidoscopic results.

THE PATCHWORK QUILT

Whether the design is simple or complex, a quilt is a major project. Even one-piece patterns need a plan, especially with regard to the colour scheme. Get hold of some graph paper (pp. 60–61) and make a few scale drawings. Even if you have set your heart on a certain pattern you still need to devise a border.

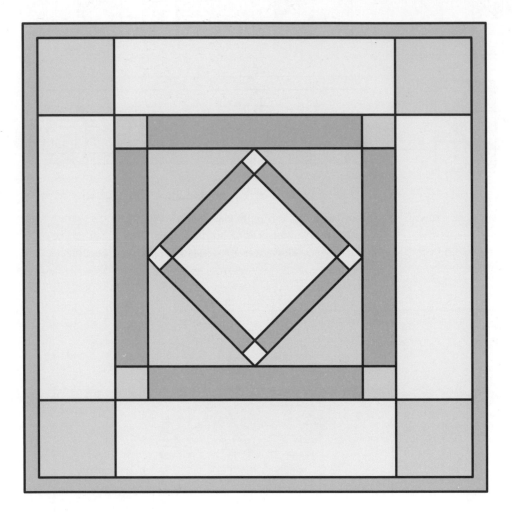

The plain-living Amish people emigrated from Germany and settled in Lancaster County, Pennsylvania in 1727. This bold *Centre Diamond* is one of their oldest designs. Large areas of plain fabric were quilted with tiny stitches (pp. 96–97), creating curled feathers, shells and stars to enliven the sober geometry.

An Amish-style block can be made any size you choose. It could easily be adapted to form one element of a 'pieced and plain' pattern. And in Amish tradition, the colours could include burgundy, olive green, russet or midnight blue.

One-shape designs

One-shape designs are an excellent showcase for clever handling of colour and light and shade effects. Their success relies on a good choice of fabrics and the ability to keep seams aligned. Using papers (p. 68) helps towards accuracy.

Mennonite sunburst Another traditional design, demanding close attention to cutting and sewing. The long diamond template has an acute angle of 45 degrees and a wide angle of 135 degrees (p. 65) see joining scheme below. Each segment consists of 49 diamonds joined at the centre with an eight-seam join (p. 71).

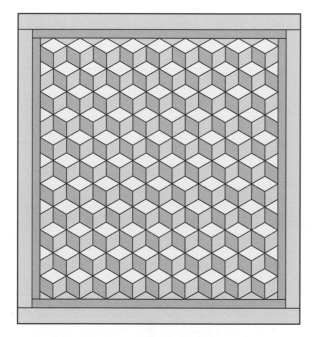

Tumbling blocks A traditional design using equal quantities of light, medium and dark fabrics in a repeat pattern that creates the illusion of falling blocks. The wide diamond template (which essentially consists of two equilateral triangles) has an acute angle of 60 degrees and a wide angle of 120 degrees. The piecing sequence can be done cube by cube; join them in rows or columns.

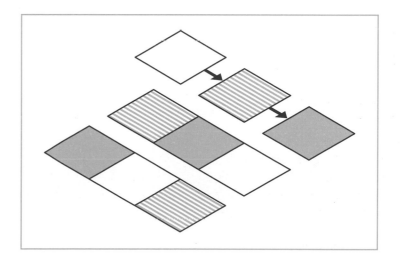

Log cabin

The most famous of all patchwork patterns, *Log Cabin* is popular for its sheer simplicity. Strips of close-woven fabric are sewn around a central square to form a larger square. No templates are needed and it can be hand- or machine-sewn, either in a single layer or attached to some type of backing. *Log Cabin* has many variations, both in piecing and arrangement of blocks, but common to all is the diagonal contrast between light and dark. By tradition, a central red square represents the hearth.

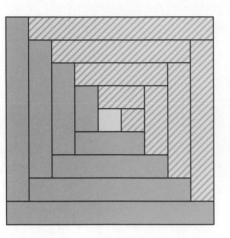

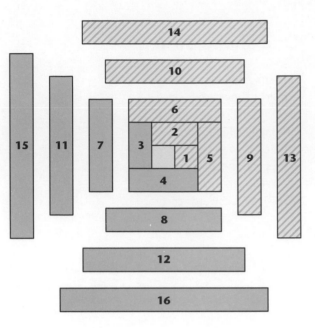

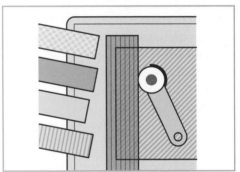

1 Prepare strips with a rotary cutter. Include 6 mm [¼ in] seam allowance on either side.

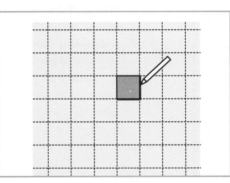

2 Mark fabric with a central square for each block and cut out with care.

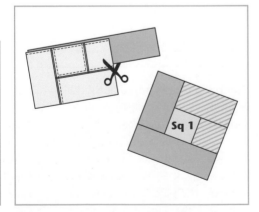

3 RS together with a 6 mm [¼ in] seam allowance, stitch first light strip to square. Trim strip to same width as square and press seam towards centre.

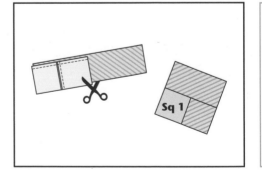

4 Attach second light strip and cut to length of previous strip plus square. Press.

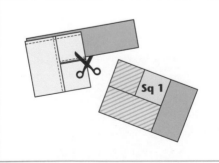

5 Take first dark strip and continue to attach anticlockwise, trimming the excess to match the pieced centre. Press.

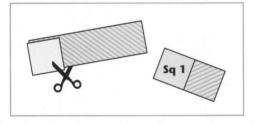

6 Attach second dark strip, trimming the excess to match pieced centre as before. Press. Continue with sequence of lights and darks until block is complete.

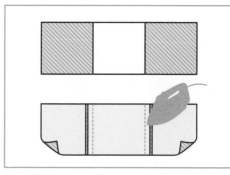

Press finished blocks carefully and check they are square. Trim if necessary, using cutting mat and ruler. All blocks must be the same size and square if the overall pattern is to work properly. Sew blocks together edge to edge in your chosen *Log Cabin* pattern.

Sunshine and shadow

Furrows

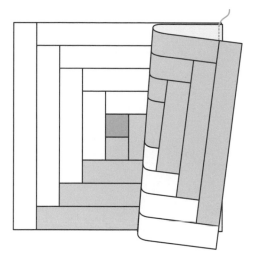

Lightning Streak

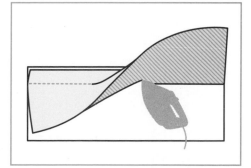

Barn Raising

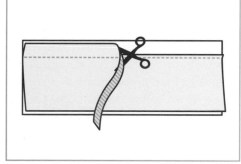

Courthouse Steps

Pressing seams

1 Patchwork seams are always pressed to one side – not open as in dressmaking – and towards the darker fabric if possible (see also p. 67).

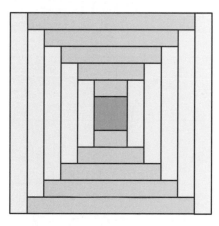

2 With a fiddly set-in or curve, press the seam open on the RS, folding the darker fabric back on itself.

3 If you must press a seam a certain way to avoid bulk, narrow the seam allowance on the dark fabric to reduce show-through.

Curved pieces

Curved pieces are more difficult to sew than straight ones but with practice (p. 75) the results can be really impressive. The templates for *Drunkard's path* and *Double axehead* are given on p. 62.

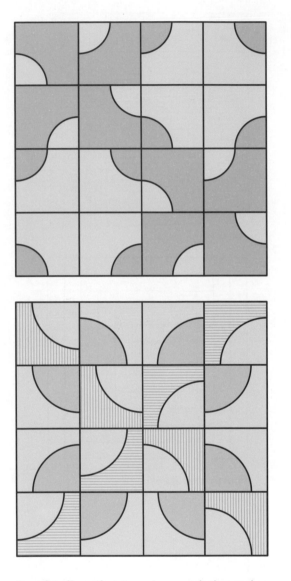

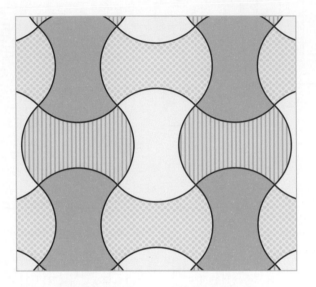

Double axehead An adaptable one-shape pattern that works on several scales. Because there are no straight lines, each and every seam must be pinned and eased, which means this pattern is more suitable for the experienced stitcher or one with a good deal of patience. Work just four patches to a block to ensure the seams lie smoothly before joining one block to the next.

Drunkard's path A two-piece patch that makes up into a 16-patch block of evenly distributed pairs. As a map of the drunkard's zigzag progress, it looks best in two plain colours; closely woven cotton being the most suitable fabric. However this pattern can be elaborated with the 'path' picked out in a single shade, framing the remaining pieces cut from five or six other colours or prints. The result looks like stained glass.

Clamshell pattern

Silks or satins in pale pastels have a totally different character from brightly coloured 'scrap' cottons, and yet both are well suited to the shell pattern. Arrange solid colours and prints in set rows or sew them together at random. The template is on p. 62.

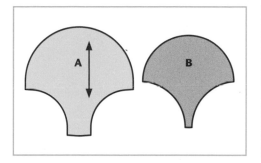

1 Trace A and B on to thin card and cut fabric out using A.

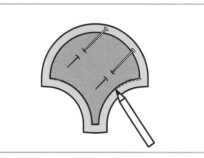

2 Pin B on to RS and outline lower curves with fabric marker.

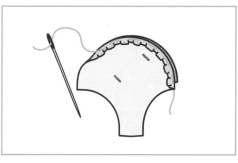

3 Turn to WS and tack [baste] small folds guided by the upper curve.

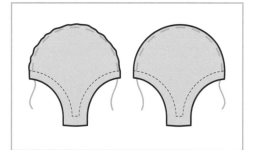

4 Remove B and press on RS to hold curve. Prepare all the shapes this way before assembling them.

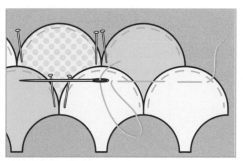

5 Pin shells in staggered rows on a sheet of board, fitting upper curves to markings on lower curves. Tack [baste] together horizontally.

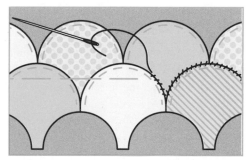

6 Unpin tacked [basted] rows from board and slip stitch together around the upper curves.

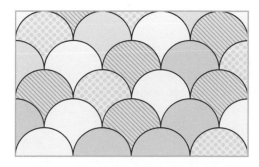

7 Remove tacking [basting] from stitched areas but not from any unstitched edges until they are finally folded and finished.

8 Using the board as in 5, turn the shells sideways. Fit upper curves into markings on lower curves and tack [baste] together before slip stitching as in 6.

Picture quilts

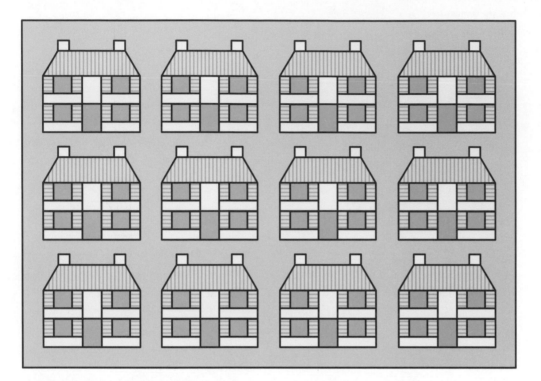

House A variation on the traditional Schoolhouse, work this version in solid colours, stripes or small checks. The plain background is pieced in a combination of sashing (pp. 76–7) and geometric shapes.

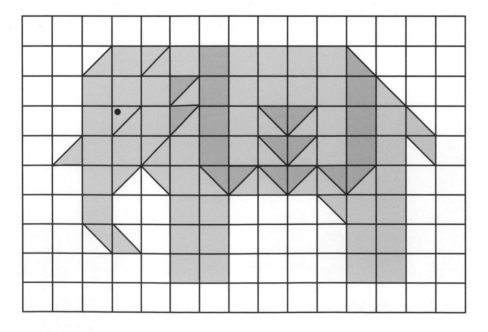

Elephant As this plan shows, an elephant can be effectively created from simple squares and triangles. As a finishing touch, you could appliqué the eye, toenails and a tufted tail (p. 94).

Use graph paper to draft other pictorial designs from geometric shapes, as shown opposite and on p. 86. Make them big and bold; they look great on children's quilts and cushions.

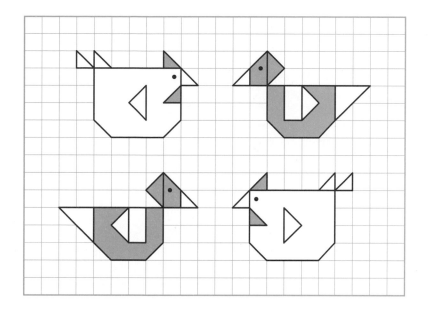

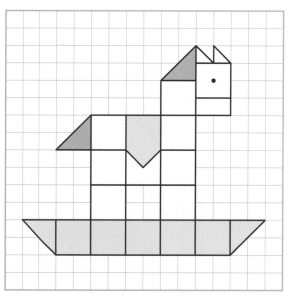

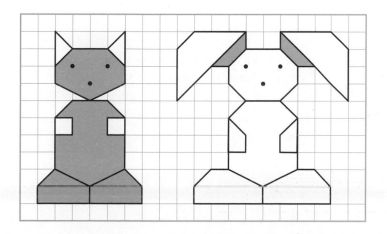

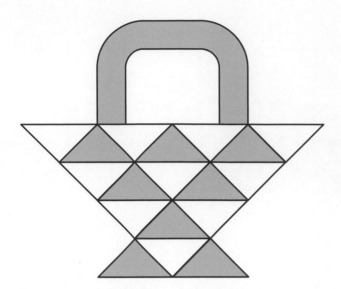

Basket A much-loved traditional block, worked in a series of triangles with an appliquéd handle cut from a single piece of fabric.

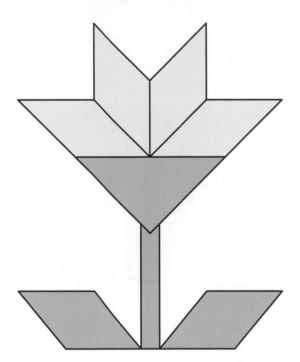

Tulip or lily Another traditional design, consisting of diamond, triangle and an appliquéd strip for the stem.

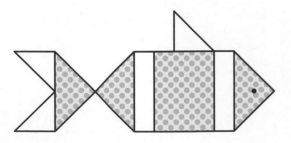

Fish Use silk, satin or metallic fabric for a shimmering effect.

PART THREE:
ASSEMBLING THE QUILT

A BASIC BORDER

The edging around a quilt top can be quite plain (pp. 91–92) or worked as intricately as the top pattern itself (p. 67). It can also be used, like sashing (pp. 76–7), to harmonize with the colours that it frames.

This border consists of four strips with no mitring at the corners. Cut to any width, it can be used to increase the overall quilt size without making extra patchwork.

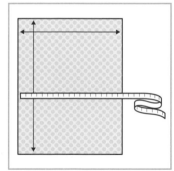 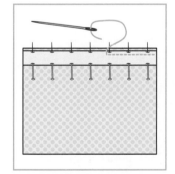 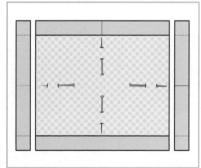 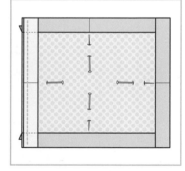

1 Measure across the middle in both directions. Cut four border strips, including a 6 mm [¼ in] seam allowance. Cut two to the length of the patchwork; the other two to the same width plus that of two border strips (see 3).

2 Take the lengthways strips first. Pin RS together to the mid-point, then outwards to either end. Tack [baste] firmly before stitching. Press.

3 Line up the shorter strips, pin and tack [baste] to the main piece as in 2.

4 Sew remaining strips straight across the ends of the first two, to form a square joint. Press.

ASSEMBLY

Inserting wadding [batting]

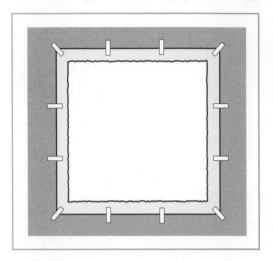

1 Press any seams in a pieced lining (p. 59). WS up, tape it to a flat surface. Centre wadding [batting] with a margin all round.

2 Having pressed the quilt top quite flat and made sure it is square, place RS up over the wadding [batting].

Pinning and tacking layers

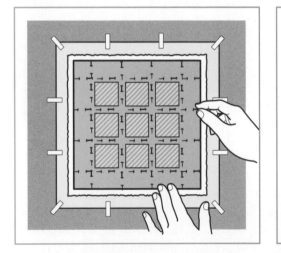

1 Pin all three layers together with long straight pins or large safety pins. You will need plenty for this stage.

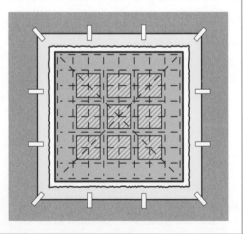

2 Knot the thread end and, starting at the centre, tack [baste] out towards the edges. First, stitch horizontally and vertically at 10 cm [4 in] intervals; then from the centre diagonally to each corner.

Machine quilting

For quilts too thick to hand-stitch: load the machine with No 40 cotton and a new 90/14 needle; set the stitch length to ten per 2.5 cm [1 in]. Choose a top thread that blends with your patchwork, and wind two bobbins with a colour to match the lining. *Do not use hand quilting thread*, as it has a wax coat that interferes with the machine's tension discs.

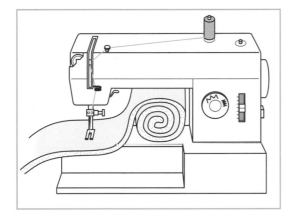

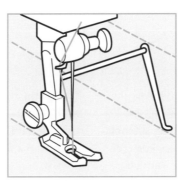

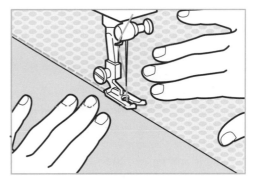

1 Roll the quilt tightly at one end and tuck under the machine throat. Begin parallel lines of stitching at the halfway point along one edge. Start and finish each line with forward and reverse stitches.

2 If you have one, use a walking/quilting foot (p. 18). A spacer guide usefully sets a regular interval between stitch lines.

3 Don't drag the quilt as you sew – this causes skipped stitches. Smooth fabric either side of the needle and go at a steady speed. Check the back for loops or puckers at the end of each line.

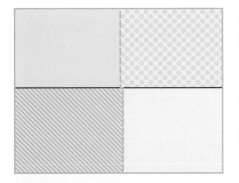

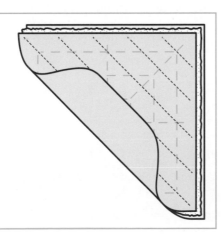

4 Ideally, seams should match but you can 'jump' a small difference across a join when 'stitching in the ditch' (when quilting follows the seams of the patchwork).

5 Roll the quilt diagonally if sewing diagonal lines. Begin at the halfway point as in 1.

Hand quilting

Tack [baste] the quilt layers together (p. 88). Hand quilters often use a frame or hoop, although many work without. Wear a metal or leather thimble on the middle finger of your sewing hand. Thread a size 8 or 10 betweens needle with wax-coated hand quilting thread, knotted at one end.

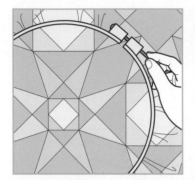

1 A quilting hoop has two rings. Separate them and lay the quilt over the inner ring. Drop the outer one over the stretched fabric and tighten the screw.

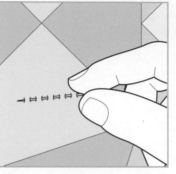

2 With one hand below the quilt for guidance, sew a series of even running stitches (p. 69) from the top. Push the head of the needle with your thimble while rocking the tip up and down through the layers.

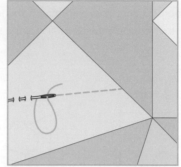

3 Pull the thread taut to define the stitch line. If the needle is hard to pull through, grip it with a flat toy balloon.

Tied [tufted] quilting

Tied [tufted] quilting is a quick way of securing layers that needs no tacking [basting]. The tufts can look very attractive: for example, you could use two colours of knitting yarn knotted together, embroidery silks [floss] or even buttons.

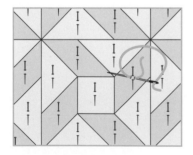

1 Mark tuft positions with long pins. Single back stitch around each pin and cut the thread.

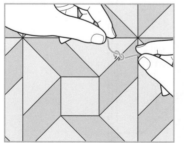

2 Tie the free ends in a double knot and trim level.

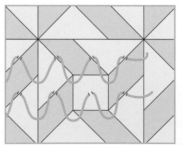

3 Alternatively, link all the back stitches with generous loops.

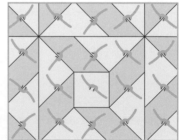

4 Cut the loops and knot each pair of ends over the central stitch.

FINISHING

Fold-over edge

This is the simplest finish of all. Trim top, wadding [batting] and lining level all round. Together, fold the lining fabric and wadding [batting] back 15 mm [⅝ in]. Pin or tack [baste] to hold them in position if necessary. Turn top edge under once to meet folded edge of lining. Slip stitch top and lining together.

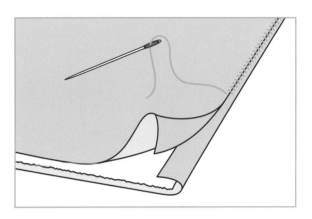

Self-bound edge

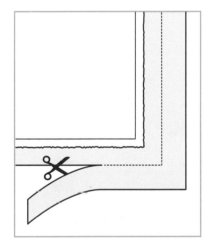

1 With top and wadding [batting] already trimmed level, cut lining with an allowance of 2.5–5 cm [1–2 in] all round.

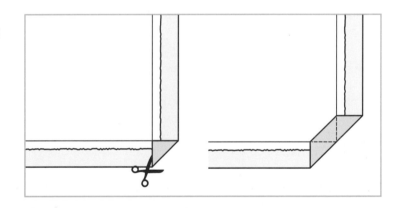

2 Fold, cut and fold again each corner of the lining, in preparation for mitring.

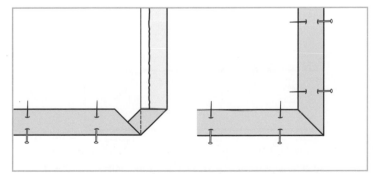

3 Fold the lining upwards to meet the quilt top and form a self-binding. Turn raw edges under and pin adjacent sides, with corners meeting in a neat diagonal line.

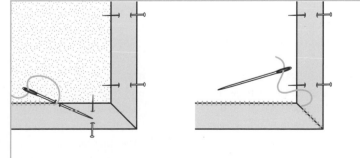

4 Using matching thread, slip stitch the binding to the quilt top all round, closing each mitred corner as you go.

Straight bound edge

Measure quilt both ways and add 5 cm [2 in] to length and width. On the grain (p. 14), cut four binding strips 3.8–5 cm [1½–2 in] wide. Press a turning of 6 mm [¼ in] down one side of each strip.

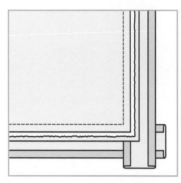 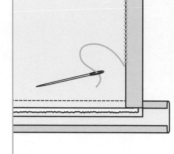 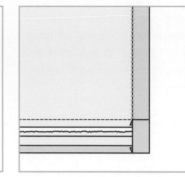 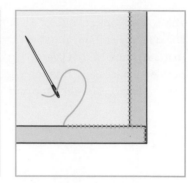

1 RS together, align unturned edge with raw edge of quilt top. Machine stitch together with a 6 mm [¼ in] seam allowance. Prepare all four sides like this.

2 Fold pressed edge of binding over to WS. Pin and slip stitch first length to lining fabric, covering initial stitch line.

3 Fold in edge of adjacent binding. Trim away bulk if necessary.

4 Fold binding up to cover all raw edges. Slip stitch to lining fabric as in 2 and close squared corner. Repeat around quilt.

Bias bound edge

Bias binding is often used on quilted items that cannot be neatened by turning. It can be homemade from steam-pressed bias strips to your chosen width, or bought readymade in various widths and materials.

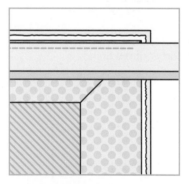 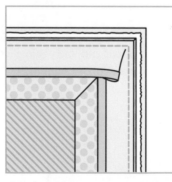

1 Press open one side of the bias binding. RS together, align with raw edge of quilt top. Pin and stitch along fold line of binding.

2 Carry on sewing right round the quilt. The bias (p. 14) will stretch around the corners as shown on the *Rose of Sharon* quilt opposite.

Signing your quilt

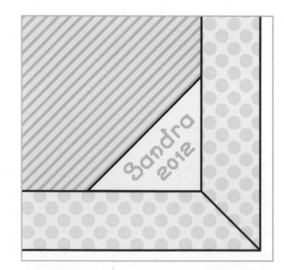

As a finishing touch, embroider your name and the date on to the quilt. Work it into the border, or make a separate label that can be slipstitched to the lining or bound neatly into one corner, as shown here.

PART FOUR:
APPLIQUÉ AND QUILTING

APPLIQUÉ

Appliqué means 'applied' and describes the technique of stitching one fabric on top of another, either by hand or machine. Practical and decorative, it is widely used on clothes and soft furnishings. As a fabric art, appliqué goes back to the Ancient Egyptians and is now firmly established among quiltmakers.

The *Rose of Sharon* pattern frequently appeared on American bridal quilts. Complex appliqué like this involves careful planning; the plans show the stitching order for the rose motif. Repeat shapes are cut from paper or card templates, based on original drafts on graph paper. When it is finished, always press appliqué RS down on a padded surface.

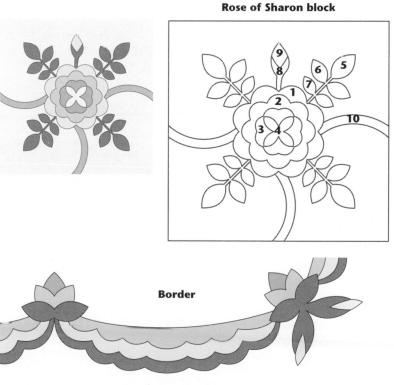

Rose of Sharon block

Border

Cutting out and attaching appliqué

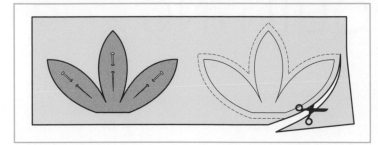

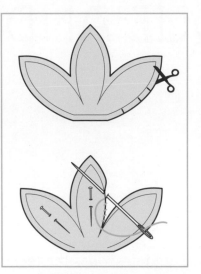

1 Pin template to fabric and trace round with a fabric marker. Cut shape out with 6 mm [¼ in] seam allowance; omit allowance if planning to oversew (3).

2 Make small clips on curves for a smooth edge when slip stitching appliqué to base fabric (p. 69). With size 8 sharps needle and waxed quilting thread, turn seam allowance under with needle tip as you sew.

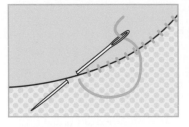

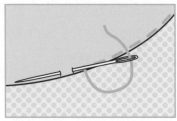

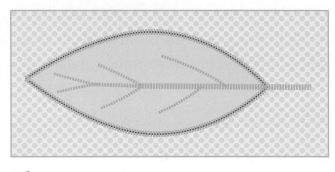

3 You can oversew the raw edges of your shape directly on to the base fabric. Sew stitches close together if the edges fray.

4 Running stitch can be used for attaching non-fraying material such as felt.

5 Appliqué by machine offers a wide choice of stitch effects, including zigzag and satin stitch.

Outlining with braid and cord

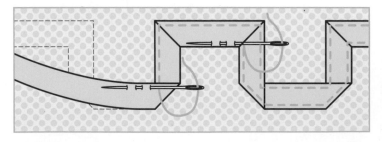

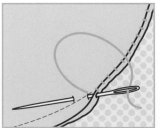

1 Add emphasis to applied shapes by outlining them. Braid may be sewn on by hand or machine; however, it must be done with precision and no wrinkles.

2 Cord defines curves where braid cannot. It is couched down by hand sewing. The needle passes through the cord and picks up threads at the edge of the appliqué, pulling the two together.

Hawaiian appliqué

A formalized style of appliqué, where intricate designs are cut from folded paper and transferred to a plain coloured fabric. The fabric is cut out and sewn on to a white background. Quilting afterwards outlines the pattern in multiple rows known as kapa lau.

The template starts as a square piece of paper folded in half twice and then a third time on the diagonal, which will produce eight sections. A design is drawn on one triangular section and traced on to a section of fabric folded in the same way.

With the layers of fabric pinned together, the appliqué is cut out with very sharp scissors along the traced lines. When opened, it is pinned and tacked [basted] firmly to the white base fabric. Working from the centre outwards, the appliqué edge is rolled under by 3 mm [1/8 in] and neatly oversewn clockwise with matching waxed thread.

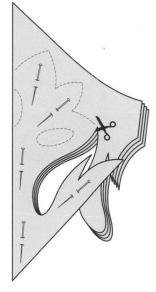

ANTIQUE CUT OUTS

Two mid-nineteenth-century templates cut from contemporary New York State newspapers and used to create appliquéd designs for a bridal quilt that sadly remained unfinished.

QUILTING

Quilting is the process of joining the three layers of a wadded quilt together with a stitched pattern that gives texture to a plain surface.

Quilting became a cottage industry in nineteenth-century Britain, and certain motifs – like the conical shells shown right – became stock-in-trade. Craftsmen and women set themselves up to stitch quilts for others, even taking their frames to work in customers' houses. In America, the same task gave rise to more lively social gatherings, called quilting bees.

Stitching method

An introduction to hand quilting and the necessary equipment appears on p. 90.

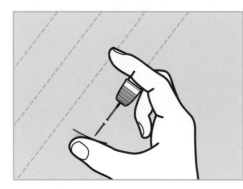

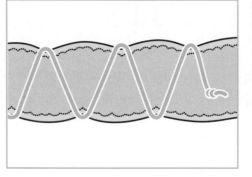

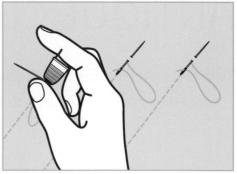

1 Following the markings, stitch rows of small, even running stitches through all three layers. In the past, rows were regularly stitched no more than 5 cm [2 in] apart to ensure the filling stayed in place.

2 Stitches will get smaller with practice. Few achieve the ideal of ten stitches per 2.5 cm [1 in]; six is more realistic. Pull the thread taut enough to make indentations in both surfaces.

3 To help work evenly across a large quilt, it's a good idea to have several needles threaded up at once.

Some traditional stitched details

1 An Amish roundel and quilt border pattern (p. 78).

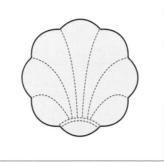

2 A scallop shell motif from Northumberland, in north-east England.

3 A Jacobean-style corner piece, reminiscent of crewel embroidery.

A PIPED [CORDED] EDGE

Piping [cording], sandwiched securely between the top and backing fabric, gives a neat, firm edge to finely stitched quilting. The cord itself should be pre-shrunk. It comes in various sizes; use the one appropriate for your fabric. Piping must be supple enough to bend around corners and so it is encased in bias-cut strips.

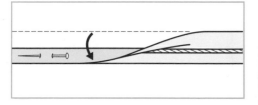

1 Pin the cord into the bias-cut strip and tack [baste], leaving a 15 mm [5/8 in] seam allowance.

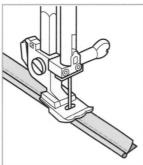

2 Machine stitch as close as possible to the cord. Use a piping or zipper foot for best results.

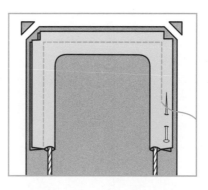

3 Raw edges aligned, tack [baste] and machine stitch piping [cording] around RS of quilt top, ends overlapping 15 mm [5/8 in]. Trim bulk to give neatly turned corners. Fold raw edges inwards so cord stands proud. Turn in raw edges of the backing to just below curve of cord. Slip stitch folded edge of backing to the piping [cording] fabric.

SASHIKO

The Japanese embroidery Sashiko lends itself to quilting because it uses a long running stitch. Around three centuries ago, Japanese men wore indigo-dyed jackets constructed from two layers of fabric. The women stitched these layers together for durability, and so the familiar Sashiko patterns evolved.

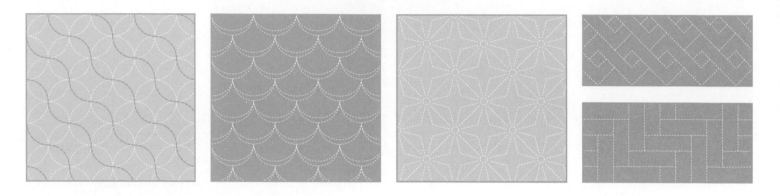

Here are five traditional Sashiko designs: horizontal and vertical lines are usually stitched first and then the diagonals; any remaining shapes are done last. Sashiko needles are 5 cm [2 in] long with a uniform shaft. The stitch count is five or six to 2.5 cm [1 in]. Use thick white thread – such as perle [pearl] embroidery twist – on dark blue cotton fabric for an authentic look.

This quilted purse uses a Sashiko pattern that includes decorative glass beads.

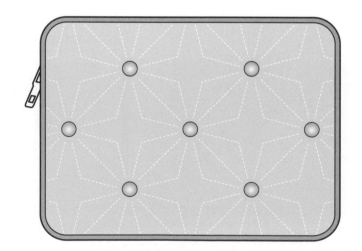

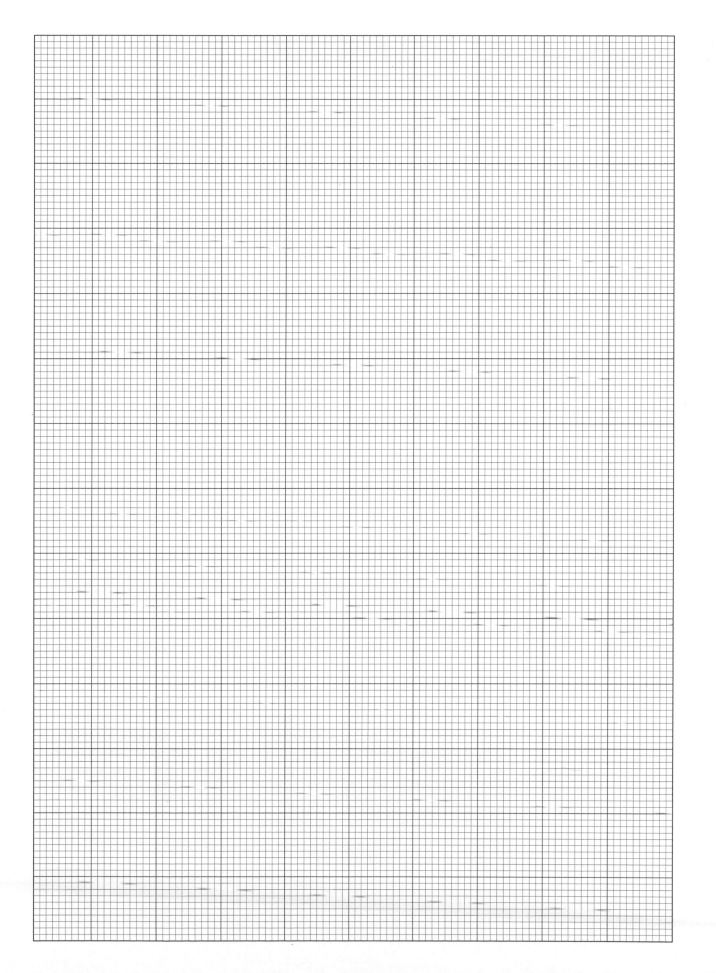

DISPLAY AND AFTERCARE

Display

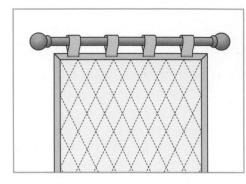

To display your work as a wall hanging, maybe in an exhibition, you must have some way of suspending it. Construct a row of tabs from fabric that matches the quilt border. Oversew the base of each tab firmly to the fabric backing, or attach with strips of Velcro so that you can easily re-convert the quilt into a bed cover. Sew the soft, looped half of the Velcro to the quilt itself, and sew the hooked half to the tab.

Any unframed fabric that is not behind glass will inevitably collect dust, which in turn can attract damp and insect pests. Vacuum clean your hangings regularly and take them down to shake outdoors from time to time. Small samplers of finely stitched quilting can be box framed to keep them clean. A roundel of Welsh or Amish design, quilted on plain fabric, shows up beautifully with the right light on it.

Aftercare

Look for the care symbols on any fabric that you buy; the manufacturer's care label appears on the bolt and if possible, ask for a care ticket to take away with you. Other points of reference are your own washing machine and tumble dryer manuals. These give details of all the washing and drying programs.

Synthetic wadding [batting] is machine washable and can be tumble dried; make certain the quilt top and backing can be treated the same. On the other hand, cotton wadding [batting] should always be pre-shrunk unless you want an antique effect – some quilters use it straight from the roll deliberately because when they wash the finished quilt, it will dry with a puckered appearance typical of the quilts of the past.

If you have lightweight woollens or silk in your patchwork, and you want to wash it either by hand or machine, choose soap flakes or a liquid for delicates. The cleansing agents in liquid soaps are designed to work at low temperatures and won't leave a powdery deposit. Test strong colours (especially reds) for colourfastness and if in any doubt dry clean the quilt. Woollen or wool-mix fabrics of any kind should always be rinsed in warm water. Use the machine-washable wool setting on your machine, not the low-temperature or hand-wash program that delivers a cold rinse.

Tumble dryers are large contributors to accidental shrinkage, and some fabrics are better left to dry without any heat at all.

Lift your quilt from the washing machine and use a clean towel to remove excess water. Lay the quilt to dry flat or drape it over a drying rack. If necessary, iron fabrics according to the recommended heat setting. Take extra care with trimmings; nylon lace, metallic threads and plastic sequins will shrivel at the touch of a hot iron.

When storing household linen, put items away clean, dry, and unstarched (silverfish love starch). Dust, dirt and perspiration harm and discolour fibres of all kinds, and both moths and moulds feed readily on dirt. Keep quilts folded neatly in chests and cupboards, or inside zipped cotton covers for long-term storage. Shake them out occasionally and refold a different way to prevent permanent creases. Avoid the risk of mould or mildew by never storing fabrics in poorly ventilated, damp or humid surroundings such as lofts, cellars or neglected cupboards. Low-powered heaters and dehumidifiers help to combat damp and condensation.

While you may see clothes moths in flight if they are present in your house, it is their larvae that make the holes in fabric. There are pleasant alternatives to camphor mothballs, such as cedarwood blocks and lavender bags, although these will need to be renewed. Moths not only lay their eggs on wool but can ruin silk, fur or feathers. Check storage places regularly; keep disturbing the moths' potential habitat and they won't settle.

TERMS AND ABBREVIATIONS

Appliqué   Technique of stitching one fabric on top of another

Backing   The quilt lining

Basting (Tacking)   Temporary stitches made with running stitch

Batting (Wadding)   Padding in the centre layer of a quilt

Betweens   Needles for fine stitching and quilting

Bias   Any diagonal line between lengthwise and crosswise grains

Block   Pieced units sewn separately and later assembled into an overall pattern

Border   Fabric edging or frame added to the top layer of a quilt

Fat quarter   Half yard of fabric cut off the bolt then cut in half again along the lengthwise grain

Felt   Non-woven fabric made from compressed fibres

Filling   Padding sewn between quilt top and backing

Fusible web   Iron-on synthetic bonding material

Grain   Direction in which the warp and weft threads lie

Hem   Folded and stitched edge, to prevent fraying

Isometric paper   Paper printed in a grid of equilateral triangles

Latticing   Narrow strips used to separate quilt blocks. Also called 'sashing'

Mitre   Corner pieces joined at an angle of 45 degrees

Muslin   Translucent loose-woven cotton fabric

Nap   Texture or design that runs in one direction only

Notch   Small triangular cut-outs in the seam allowance, for aligning pieces when sewing

Patch   A shaped piece of fabric

Patchwork   Fabric shapes or patches sewn together in a set design

Perle [Pearl] thread   Cotton embroidery twist

Piecing   Joining fabric shapes or patches together

Pile   Soft raised surface on velvet, corduroy etc (see Nap)

Post   Small square connecting sashing/lattice strips

Press   Often used to mean 'iron' but more strictly involves steam and a pressing cloth

Presser foot   Holds fabric flat while the machine needle makes stitches

Quilt   Bed cover consisting of two layers of fabric with padding sewn or tied between

Quilting   Action of stitching the three layers of a quilt together

Quilting hoop   Portable frame for holding a portion of quilt while stitching

RS   Right side of fabric

Rotary cutter   Cuts strips and several layers of fabric at once.

Sashiko   Traditional Japanese type of embroidery

Sashing   Narrow strips used to separate quilt blocks. Also called 'latticing'

Seam allowance   Distance between the cut edge and the seam line

Seam ripper   Tool for removing machine stitching

Selvedge [Selvage]   Solid edge of a woven fabric

Seminole   Strip-pieced technique often used for borders

Setting in   Fitting one piece into an angle formed by two others already joined

Sharps   General sewing needles

Slip stitch   Attaches a folded edge to a flat surface

String   Technique of creating a fabric from strips

Strip   Technique of pattern building based on strips of fabric rather than blocks

Tacking [basting]   Temporary stitches made with running stitch

Template   An outline guide for tracing and cutting

Tied [tufted]   Method of securing quilt layers with knots of thread

Top   Patterned top layer of a patchwork quilt

WS   Wrong side of fabric

Wadding [batting]   Padding in the centre layer of a quilt

Warp   Runs lengthwise, parallel to the selvedge [selvage]

Weft   Runs at right angles to the selvedge [selvage]

CROSS STITCH

Cross stitch is one of the oldest forms of hand embroidery, popular all over the world, and it is little wonder that it remains so. Not only is it easy to learn – cross stitch is usually the first embroidery stitch taught to children – but it's quickly arranged into patterns, pictures and letters by following grid charts where each square represents a single stitch. The pleasure in achievement can become quite addictive as the design grows and different colours are added.

The essentials of counted cross stitch are set out here with plenty of illustrations to guide you, and a basic range of free-style embroidery stitches has been added in a supplement to the counted thread method. This is a refresher for those who first learned to cross stitch years ago and would like to pick it up again. There are sections on equipment and various threads and fabrics, as well as advice on how to read charts and create your own, including numerous motifs and alphabets for you to use. The terminology used is UK-standard, together with the relevant US terms in square brackets [ ] to make this a practical guide for all readers.

The art of cross stitch dates back at least as far as the 6th or 7th century CE when it was used to decorate household linens with floral or geometric patterns, worked simply in black or red thread. Folk costumes, especially from northern and eastern Europe, are often decorated with similar traditional designs; medieval Assisi work and Tudor blackwork were beautiful, intricate developments of the same technique. Later came the familiar multicoloured sampler, which served several purposes: to record patterns or motifs in the absence of pattern books; to teach children how to stitch; and finally to demonstrate a young woman's prowess with the needle.

Nowadays, we happily incorporate cross stitch designs into many items, from greetings cards to buttons, bookmarks, pot covers and paperweights; while larger projects – including elaborate pre-printed kits – are stitched with skill and patience, hopefully to be framed as future family heirlooms.

PART ONE:
EQUIPMENT AND MATERIALS

NEEDLES AND FABRICS

Needles are manufactured in various thicknesses for different uses. The following chart is a general guide to the size of needle suitable for cross stitch on aida or evenweave fabrics. The higher the number, the finer the needle. Dimensions may vary slightly between manufacturers.

NEEDLE SIZE	FABRIC	NEEDLE LENGTH	EYE LENGTH
18	6 count aida / 10 count evenweave	48 mm	10.0 mm
20	8 count aida	44 mm	9.0 mm
22	11 count aida / 22-25-27 count evenweave	40 mm	8.0 mm
24	14 count aida / 28 count evenweave	36 mm	7.5 mm
26	16 count aida / 32 count evenweave	33 mm	6.5 mm
28	18 count aida / 36-55 count evenweave	28 mm	5.5 mm

EQUIPMENT

Cross stitch uses relatively little equipment, leaving you free to build a collection of the beautiful threads available (see rear cover photograph).

A Needles

B Fabric

C Thread (including tacking thread)

D Dressmaking shears

E Embroidery scissors

F Thimble

G Laying tool: a small pointed stick of metal or wood for smoothing and straightening threads as you stitch (a large blunt yarn needle will do)

H Masking and double-sided tape

I Embroidery marker pencil

J Embroidery chalk pencil

K Carbon paper for tracing designs

L Graph paper for charting

M Magnifying lamp

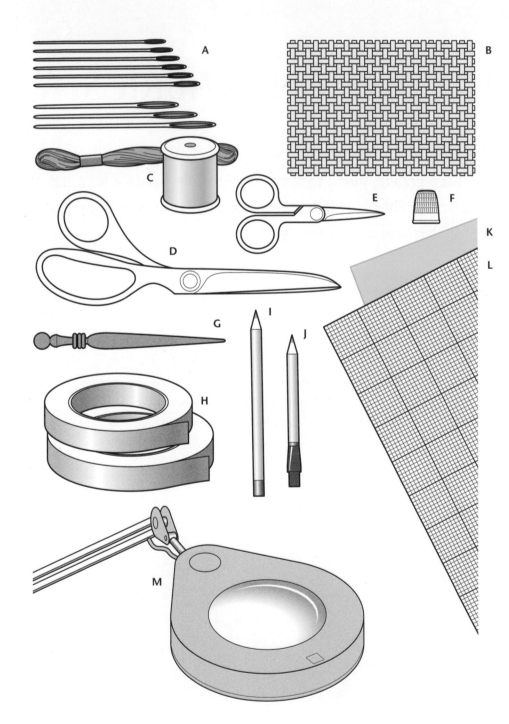

WORKING WITH HOOPS AND FRAMES

Hoops and frames are not essential equipment but they do keep the fabric taut and smooth and make it easier to see how your work is progressing.

Embroidery hoops consist of an inner and an outer ring made of wood or plastic. The fabric is first placed over the inner ring and the outer one is fastened around both by tightening a metal screw.

A hoop or frame can also be mounted on a stand, which then leaves both hands free for stitching. Many people find that stabbing the needle up and down through the fabric, with one hand above and one below, is more comfortable than hand-holding their embroidery, and it helps reduce any pain or cramp in the wrists and fingers.

On the whole, unless your project is quite small-scale, it is better to use a frame than an embroidery hoop. Instead of having to reposition the hoop as you go, the entire work is stretched between two bars.

Hoop marks left on a finished project can be avoided by first wrapping both inner and outer rings with bias binding or by placing tissue paper between the outer ring and the embroidery (tear the tissue away from the stitching area). Remove the hoop when you are not working.

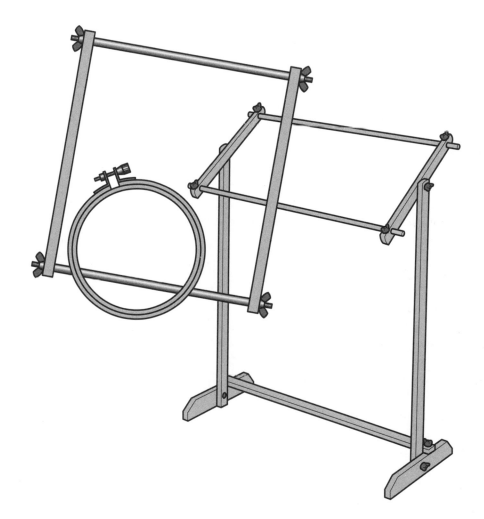

NEEDLES

Cross stitch is worked with blunt-tipped tapestry needles designed to glide through the holes in the fabric weave without splitting the threads. They have long oval eyes (see chart p. 103) that will take multiple strands of embroidery cotton [floss] as well as craft threads like perle [pearl] cotton and tapestry wool. Here are other useful additions to your needle case:

Blunt-tipped

Pointed

Sharps Medium-length pointed needles with a round eye, for general sewing with ordinary cotton or polyester thread.

Embroidery or crewel Pointed like sharps but with long oval eyes like tapestry needles.

Chenille Sharp points and long oval eyes but larger than a crewel, for use on heavy fabrics.

Milliner's needles (also called 'straws') With round eyes, even shaft and sharp point.

Bodkins Large blunt-tipped needles, sometimes flat, with an eye big enough to take cord, elastic or ribbon through loops and casings.

Eyes are either round or oval; round ones are the smallest and long oval the largest. Although a small needle helps with fine work, if the eye is too tight around the thread or yarn, it will be difficult to pull through the fabric and could fray the thread in the process.

Most needles are nickel plated; however, the quality varies. They sometimes become discoloured and may make marks on your work if left stuck in the fabric, so put them away when you have finished. Gold and platinum plated needles will not discolour or rust but they are more expensive.

Some people keep a tiny emery cushion packed firmly with sand, which acts as an abrasive to clean the needles when stuck into the cushion.

THREADS

Most embroidery threads can be used in cross stitch. They are available in many forms, in balls, on spools, or in skeins and hanks.

Stranded cotton [floss] Often called 'silk' and the most commonly used thread. It consists of six divisible strands in a small skein.

Perle [pearl] cotton Shiny 2-ply twisted thread. Unlike stranded cotton, it cannot be separated into strands. However, it is available in various thicknesses.

Soft cotton 5-ply unmercerized cotton twist, non-divisible like perle [pearl]. During manufacture it is combed to produce a soft thread that is easy to work with. This makes it a popular choice for young children learning cross stitch. Its matt finish and soft colours also suit antique-style projects such as samplers.

Stranded rayon Hi-gloss six-stranded thread [floss].

Z-twist rayon Glossy 4-ply twist, spun clockwise.

Metallic threads A wide range to choose from. Slightly abrasive, tending to fray at the ends, these call for a large-eyed needle to make a bigger hole in the cloth and reduce the drag on both thread and fabric. For this reason it is best to work with short lengths.

Space-dyed (or variegated) threads Factory-dyed in multiple colours, or in shades of a single colour, at regular intervals along the thread.

Hand-dyed threads Dyed by hand using one or more colours, possibly neither light- nor colour-fast.

Choose threads in natural light because artificial lighting intensifies certain colours and dulls others. The fibres that you choose are equally important for the texture or finish of your embroidery and you should always bear in mind the end use of whatever you make.

You can buy shade cards, including actual thread samples, from major manufacturers such as DMC, Coats Anchor, Madeira and Kreinik. They are also obtainable from online needlecraft suppliers.

When using a twist thread, always thread your needle directly from the ball before cutting off the length required. This ensures that the twist of the thread goes in the same direction every time, giving an even appearance to your stitches.

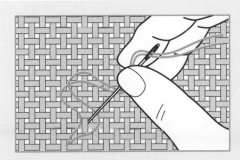

'Railroading' is the technique of separating and smoothing strands of thread as you stitch. As you push your needle into the fabric to make a stitch, pass it between two strands.

FABRICS AND THREAD COUNTS

The background texture and colour provided by your fabric is important. The most widely used fabrics for cross stitch are evenweave and aida, and both come in ranges of neutral tones and colours.

Aida

This block weave fabric is favoured by beginners because of its regular construction and visible stitch holes. It also has a stiffer finish for hand-held work. It is worth noting that unworked areas have a distinct texture compared with evenweave.

If the pattern contains fractional stitches (p. 120), you will have to make an additional hole between the existing ones by stitching into the solid section of the block weave.

5-, 6- or 8-count A low-count aida for use by children, sometimes called Binca canvas.

11-count Many find that they can work on this when the more usual 14-count becomes too hard on the eyes.

14-count Easy to work and used in more commercial designs than any other fabric.

16-count Gives scope for greater detail than 14-count.

18-count An aida for detailed work. Stitch a small sample before launching upon a large project as you may find this count too demanding for comfort.

22-count Another aida for really fine work. Traditionally used for Hardanger and also ideal for small projects such as pot lids, paperweights and coasters.

Evenweave

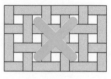

An evenweave is any natural or man-made fabric having the same number of threads per inch (2.5 cm) counted vertically and horizontally; this keeps the cross stitches square and even. It is frequently made either of linen, such as Belfast (32-count) and Cashel (28-count) or – less expensively – of cotton, such as Linda (27-count) and Hardanger (22-count).

Evenweave threads are usually of uniform thickness, though the pure linens are more random. Cross stitch is worked over two threads, so you will be stitching into alternate holes.

The *greater the thread count* per inch, sometimes given as HPI (holes per inch), the *finer the cloth* and the *smaller your stitches* will be. A 22-count evenweave will yield 11 cross stitches per inch and a 32-count produces 16.

Evenweave and aida are interchangeable with the aid of a little arithmetic. So if a pattern calls for 28-count evenweave stitched over 2 threads of the fabric, use a 14-count aida and stitch into every hole instead. In the same way, you would replace 32-count evenweave with 16-count aida, and 22-count with 11-count.

Both fabrics are woven in a variety of widths and also in narrow bands with pre-stitched edges, suitable for bookmarks, cakebands, tie-backs and so on. The bands are 3–8 cm [1¾–3 in] in width.

Canvas

You can cross stitch with tapestry wool or stranded cotton [floss] on a cotton or linen canvas. There are four mesh sizes, 10-, 12-, 14- and 18-count, which are compatible with any stitch chart (count the holes in canvas work, not the threads). With a starched finish that gives a firm base to work on, canvas comes as both single thread mesh (mono) and double (duo).

The latter is also called Penelope canvas, which can be used to double your count and – like evenweave – simplifies fractional stitches. Ease the double threads apart first with a thick tapestry needle, then treat each as a single.

Plastic canvas

Plastic mesh is available in circles as well as straight-sided sheets. It is usually stitched with 4-ply or double knitting [worsted] wool over counts of 5, 7, 10 or 14 holes to the inch (2.5 cm). Being rigid, it can be pre-cut for making into items such as boxes, place mats, Christmas decorations, photo frames and key fobs.

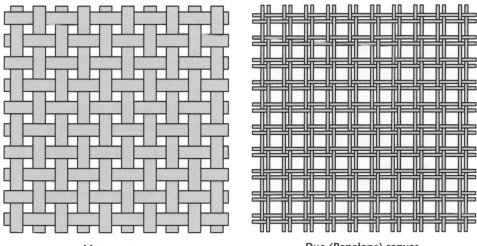

Mono canvas

Duo (Penelope) canvas

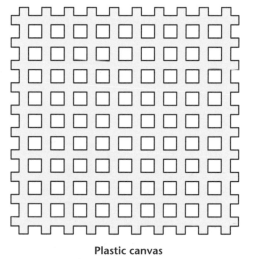

Plastic canvas

CALCULATING QUANTITIES

When calculating the amount of fabric you need for a project, add a clear margin of 10–12 cm [4–5 in] around the outer edges of the design. Allow proportionally less if the design itself is no bigger than a 10–12 cm [4–5 in] square.

A skein of embroidery cotton [floss] is approximately 7.5 m [25 feet] long. On average, people work with a 45 cm [18 in] length of cotton [floss] at a time. You will get roughly 16 working lengths of 6 strands' thickness from one skein and twice as many with it split into 3 strands. It is wise to discount one of those lengths for starting and finishing and general wastage.

CROSS STITCH CHARTS AND HOW TO READ THEM

Pattern books became very popular in Europe and America during the seventeenth century. In the early days, cross stitch patterns had only plain black squares or dots, with no colour guide. Now there is a variety of squared charts, from those that use only symbols for colours to those printed in full colour.

Here is a very simple heart-shaped motif. Each square on the chart represents two threads of evenweave fabric or one block of aida, and each stitch occupies one square.

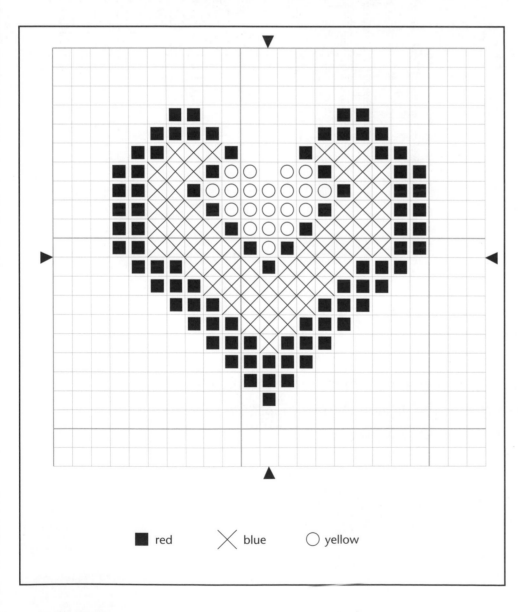

■ red   ✕ blue   ○ yellow

Design size 17w x 16h

Stitching level Beginner

Always mark the centre of each edge of the chart with a small arrowhead. Even so, it can be difficult to keep your place on a large chart. Try dividing it into a grid of manageable sections, marked with a coloured pen (see also p. 117).

Small symbols in one corner of a square stand for either a quarter-stitch or three-quarter stitch (see p. 120) and these two can also be combined within the same square. In that case, the chart will show a square divided by a diagonal. The half-stitch is generally used for shading or to lighten a colour.

CHARTING YOUR OWN DESIGN

Being able to chart your own design broadens your cross-stitching horizons considerably. The choice of subjects is limitless and with practice you will develop the knack of visualizing a finished item. Graph paper is essential. If you haven't any, you can scan or photocopy basic grids like those provided overleaf, or download graph paper in various count sizes from online needlecraft sites.

It is the number of stitches from top to bottom and side to side that fix the design size; do not forget to include any stitched background area in your calculations. Start by outlining the required number of squares on your chart. For a 30 cm (12 in) design, you will work to 168 (12x14) stitches on 14-count aida. There will be fewer stitches on 11-count: 132 (12x11) and many more stitches on 18-count: 216 (12x18).

Remember that *evenweave is worked over two threads so divide the evenweave thread count by two* before you begin to calculate the number of stitches required.

You can either colour in your chart or, if you are charting in black and white, decide on a system of symbols as a key to the colours.

Digital chartmaking

If you want to create a chart via your computer and you have the necessary software, the graphics program Adobe Photoshop can be used to convert a photograph to a counted cross-stitch pattern. There are also online charts of leading thread manufacturers' colours for you to choose from.

Cross-stitched initials vary a lot in width or depth according to the letters of the alphabet. Capitals G, M, Q, R and W are the ones to watch out for, particularly if you are working to tight margins such as a key fob or bookmark.

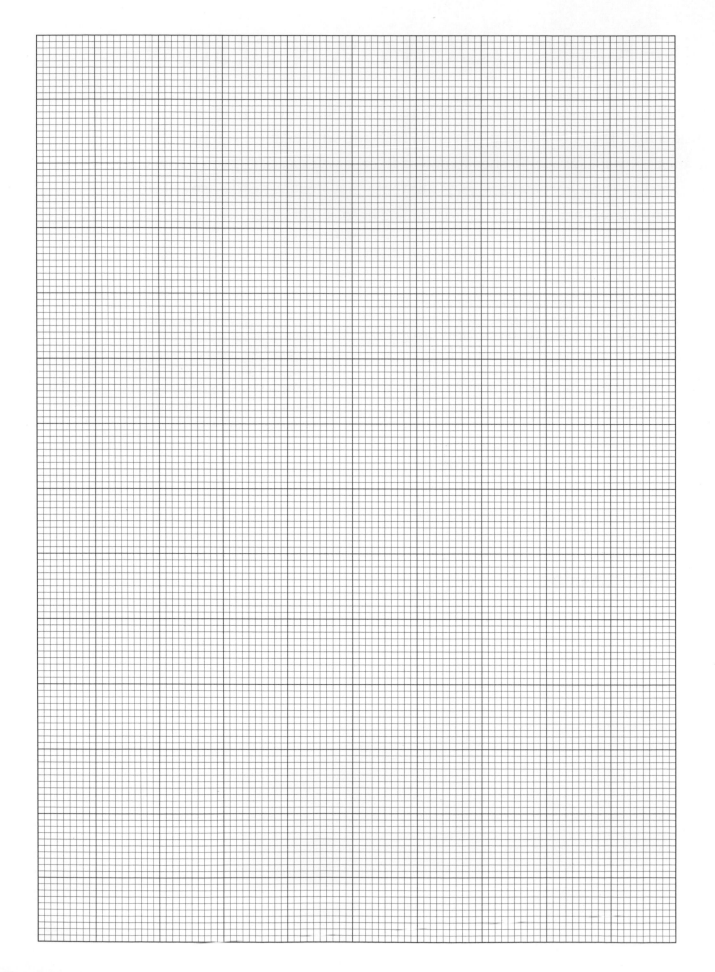

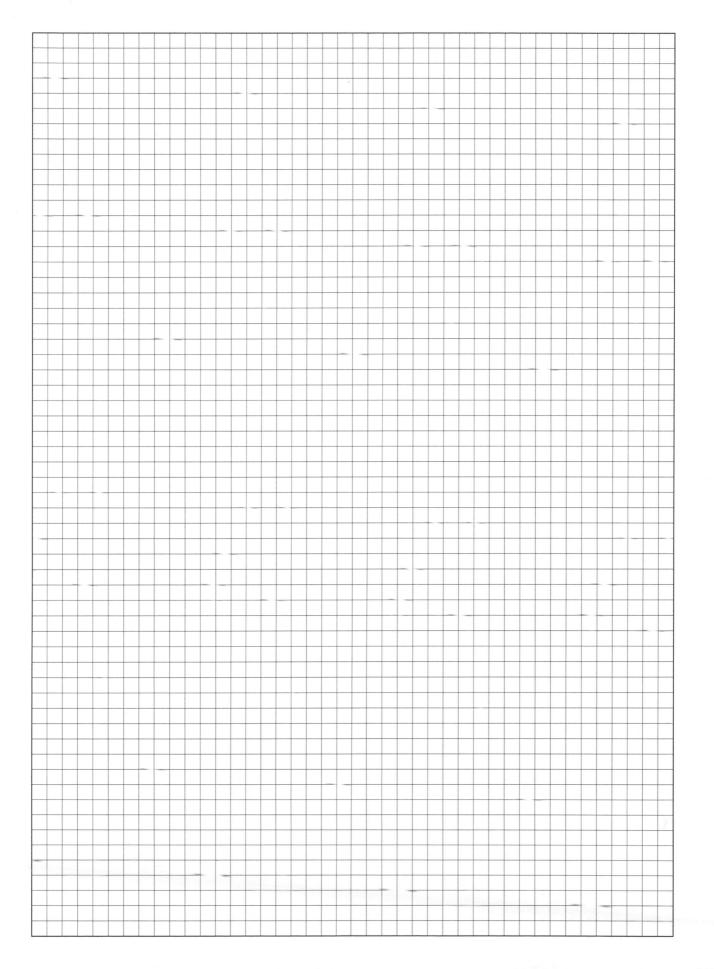

READYMADES

There are many manufactured items that you can buy from needlecraft suppliers to decorate with cross stitch, including plastic canvas for you to cut and construct to your own designs (p. 136) and ideas for box shapes as below.

Small objects like key fobs, pot lids and tasselled scissor keepers are a very encouraging way of starting – and finishing – a project (see p. 137). As gift items they can be given the personal touch of initials or a favourite motto, or stitched to match a particular colour scheme. Kits are also available for brooches, wallets, coasters, fridge magnets, handbag mirrors, paperweights, pendants and pin cushions.

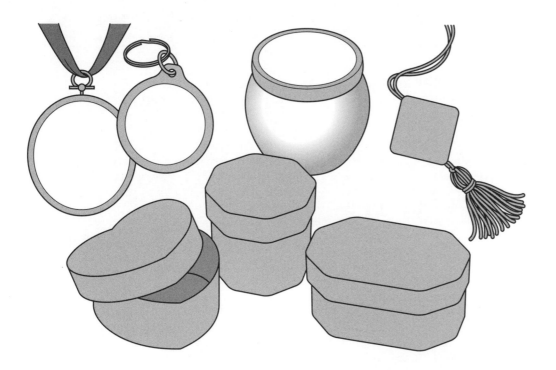

PART TWO:
CROSS STITCH METHODS AND TECHNIQUES

RECORD CARD

At the start of a project, punch a line of holes in a piece of card and loop a 7 cm [3 in] strand from each skein through a separate hole. Write the name of the project in the centre of the card and then label each hole with the appropriate manufacturer's name, shade number and chart symbol. This provides you with a quick reference while you work and a handy record once you have finished.

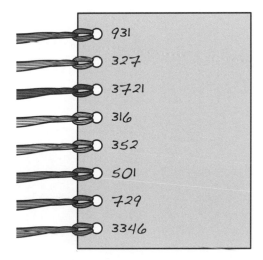

PREPARING FABRIC

Keep fabrics in a sealed bag or box and wash your hands before handling. When you have cut a new piece – removing any selvedges [selvages] in the process – check it carefully for faults in the weave and then iron it smooth under a clean, dry cloth (a piece of old sheeting will do). Stubborn creases may require steaming.

Prepare the raw edges

Linen frays very easily, so does evenweave, aida less so. But whatever fabric you use, you should prepare the raw edges in order to keep them neat and prevent your threads getting caught while you embroider. Here are some options:

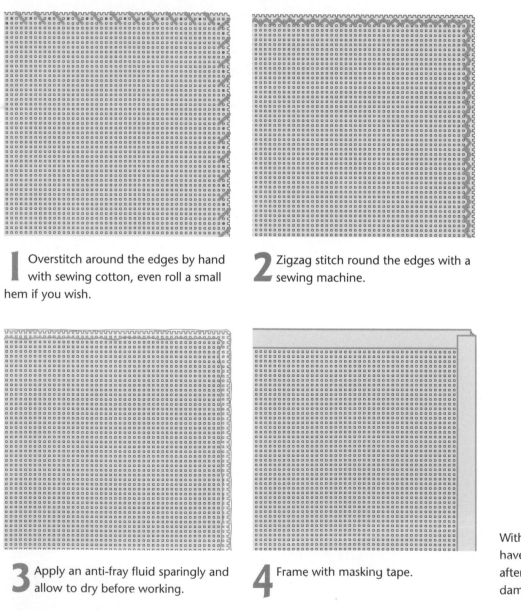

1 Overstitch around the edges by hand with sewing cotton, even roll a small hem if you wish.

2 Zigzag stitch round the edges with a sewing machine.

3 Apply an anti-fray fluid sparingly and allow to dry before working.

4 Frame with masking tape.

With 3 and 4, be aware that you will have to cut away 1 cm [½ in] all round afterwards. Chemicals and adhesives will damage the fabric in the long run.

Tacking guidelines

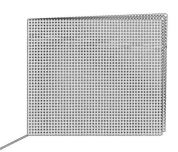

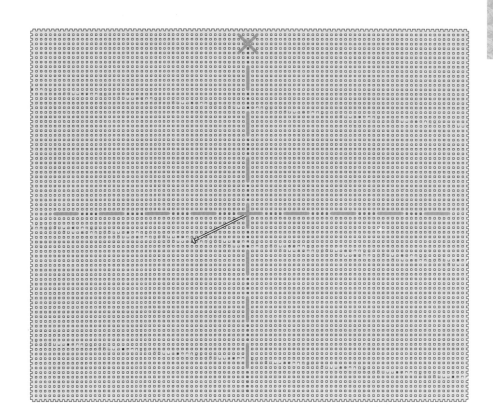

1 Fold the fabric in half twice to find the centre point, crease gently with your fingers and mark with a pin.

2 Open out and tack [baste] along the folds in a contrasting thread; this stitching corresponds to the coloured guidelines on your chart (p. 110). Use soft cotton tacking thread if possible because it is easier to remove.

Choose a place outside your stitching area and sew a large X to indicate the right side of the work and mark the top.

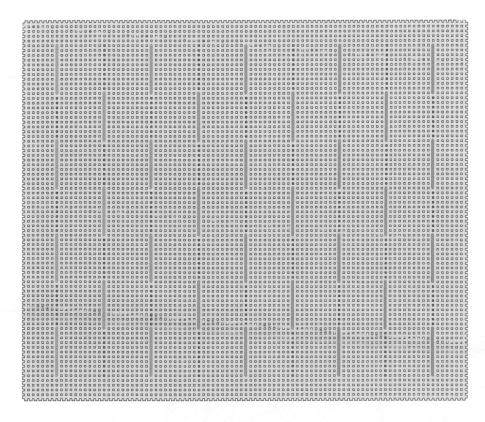

Grid making

In addition to marking the two central lines with tacking thread, you could go further and tack [baste] an entire grid based on squares of 10x10. This is worth considering if you are starting a large project since you will save time and be able to orientate yourself more easily, even working one colour at a time right through the design. The chances of counting errors are reduced because you never have to count more than ten up, down or across.

You will already have the 10x10 grid marked on your chart for cross reference (p. 110).

PREPARING THREADS

How many strands to use

As a rule, the number of strands of cotton [floss] that you sew with should match the thickness of one thread pulled out from the edge of the fabric. People generally use three or four strands on an 11-count fabric, two or three for a 14-count, and two for an 18-count.

Single strand outline

Many pictorial cross stitch designs are outlined in backstitch. This is often sewn in black (not to be confused with blackwork, p. 121) with just one or two strands of cotton [floss].

Separating and recombining stranded cotton [floss]

Multiple strands of cotton [floss] used straight from the skein can produce bumpy stitches so it is worth taking the trouble to separate the strands, smooth them straight and put them together again *in the same direction*. This will reduce twisting and tangling, and the stitches will lie better.

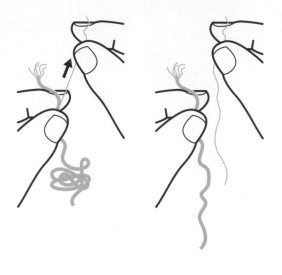

Grip one strand firmly at the top and draw your other hand down, taking the remaining threads with you until the single strand is free. The others will bunch up but won't become knotted. Finally, lay all the strands out straight and reassemble them as you wish.

Tweeding

Different coloured strands threaded into the same needle is known as tweeding. Achieved by separating strands (see above), it is a good way of introducing textural effects and also of creating extra colours without buying more; for instance, blue and pink strands will produce mauve. There is also a very fine metallic thread, known as a 'blending filament' designed for combination with ordinary stranded cotton [floss].

The blending filament and stranded cotton [floss] will not slip when the filament is threaded up as shown. The cotton [floss] is threaded up afterwards in the usual way.

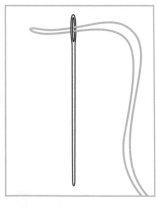

1 Loop the filament and thread it into the needle.

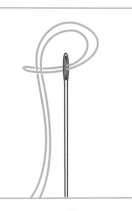

2 Thread the free ends through the loop.

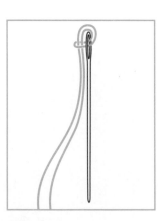

3 Pull the ends of the filament very gently to secure it in the eye of the needle.

Thread organizer

As well as creating a record card (p. 115), well-organized stitchers might like to make a similar one for use throughout the project. Cut a thread of each colour to a working length (about 45 cm [18 in]) and loop it through the punched card, where it remains ready for the needle.

Metallic threads tend to twist or break more easily, so it is advisable to cut those into shorter lengths (about 30 cm [12 in]). They also tend to unravel at the ends, which can be stopped with anti-fray fluid. Ends can be prepared in advance on the thread organizer and eventually trimmed off.

STARTING AND FASTENING OFF

Unless the design demands otherwise, stitch from the centre and work outwards, counting the squares as you go. Unless you have tacked [basted] a grid (p. 117), plan your progress to avoid long empty stretches because that's where you run the risk of miscounting. Also, carrying threads very far across the back tends to show through.

No knots

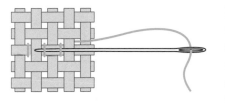

Knots at the back will appear as unsightly bumps on the front of your work when it is finally pressed and mounted. They will even pop right through the weave if it is loose enough. So, when starting out, push your needle through from the wrong side leaving a 3 cm [1.5 in] tail of thread at the back. Hold the tail against the fabric as you go and it will soon be caught down by the new stitches.

The correct way to fasten off is to run the thread under three or four wrong-side stitches, either horizontally or vertically. Whipping the end around one of those stitches helps to secure it.

Waste knots

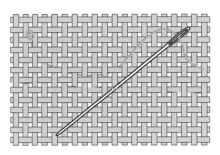

First knot the end of the thread and from the *right side* push your needle through to the back, leaving the knot on the surface of the fabric. Next, bring your needle through again about 2.5 cm [1 in] from the knot and start stitching towards it. Stab stitch steadily and be sure to completely cover the thread at the back. When that is done, trim the knot from the front.

An 'Away Waste Knot' is placed well away from the stitching and is not covered by it. When cut off, it leaves a longer tail at the back, which is threaded into a needle and woven in.

The loop start or lark's head knot

Two conditions hold for this method: first, working with an even number of strands of cotton [floss]; and second, the working length of thread should be doubled to 90 cm (36 in).

Separate one strand of cotton [floss] if you are stitching with two strands (two for four, and three for six). Fold the strand(s) double and thread the loose ends into your needle.

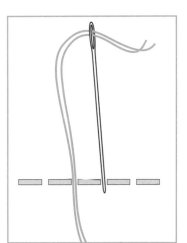

1 Stab the needle up through the fabric from the wrong to the right side and pull enough thread with it to leave a small loop at the back.

2 Make your first half cross stitch and, with the needle back on the wrong side, pass it through the waiting loop.

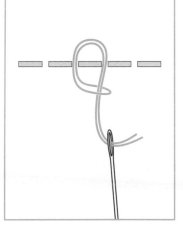

3 As you pull the thread it will draw the loop neatly against the fabric.

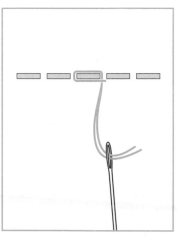

BASIC STITCHES

Cross stitch

The most important rule about cross stitch is that all the top stitches go in one direction. It doesn't matter which way as long as they are uniform. Working with separated and recombined strands (p. 118), railroading (p. 107) and smoothing your stitches with a laying tool will help.

There are two cross-stitching methods.

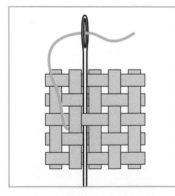

1 The traditional English method completes each X before moving on to the next.

2 The Danish method does the first legs of the Xs first, and completes them as they return along the row.

To end with all the threads in neat vertical lines on the back, stitch horizontal rows with the Danish method and vertical columns with the English.

There are also two styles of stitching. One is the 'stabbing' or 'push and pull' method. There is no alternative when working with a hoop or frame because the fabric is too taut. But if hand-holding, you can manipulate the fabric to use the 'sewing' method below.

Fractional stitches

These are quarter, half and three-quarter cross stitches, mainly used to smooth outlines and round corners. However, they can give a lighter look to an otherwise solid area, or share a square with another colour, in a variation on 'tweeding'.

The half-stitch is the same as the first leg of the Danish method shown left.

The quarter-stitch is done across one thread only if you are working on evenweave fabric; on aida it must be done as shown right.

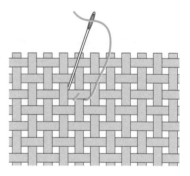

Coming up from the lower left corner, cross diagonally and insert the needle into the solid centre of the aida square. Pull the thread right through to the back.

The three-quarter-stitch on aida fabric takes the first step as for the quarter-stitch above and finishes as shown right.

Coming up from the lower right corner, cross diagonally and insert the needle into the hole top left. Pull the thread right through to the back.

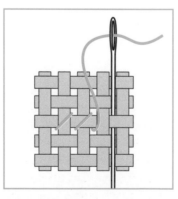

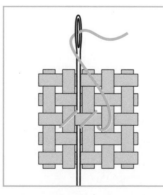

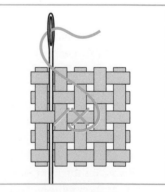

1 On the first leg, in one action, push the needle into the fabric at the top and out of the hole below.

2 Repeat for the remainder of the row.

3 Cross the last stitch diagonally, pushing the needle in at the top and out of the hole directly below.

4 Repeat to the other end of the row where all the crosses will be complete.

Backstitch

The backstitch has close links with cross stitch. It is used to define cross-stitched areas and should be done last in order to maintain an unbroken line. Some stitchers prefer to use a finer needle at this stage – it is a thin line and the number of strands is seldom more than one or two. Most often a single strand is used but it does not always have to be black; in fact, you may achieve a far more subtle and pleasing effect with a darker shade of the cross stitch filler. Start and finish by running the thread under a few cross stitches at the back of your project.

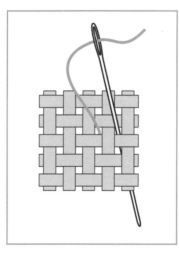

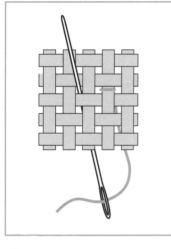

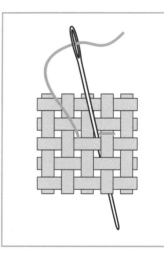

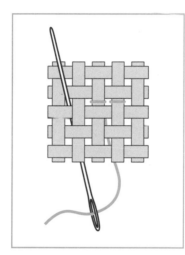

1 Push the needle in one stitch space *behind* the point where it previously came out.

2 Bring the needle back out one stitch space *in front* of the previous stitch.

3 Push it in again at the point where the previous stitch ended.

4 And bring it out one stitch space ahead of the latest stitch.

Holbein or Double Running Stitch

This is a staple stitch of blackwork. It looks like backstitch but is actually constructed from two passes of running stitch, where the second pass returns and precisely fills the gaps left by the first. This makes the back far neater than that of backstitch and ideal on its own for double-sided items such as bookmarks and Christmas tree decorations.

Blackwork

A type of decorative stitching believed to have been brought to England from Spain by Henry VIII's first wife, Catherine of Aragon. It eventually developed into the English style of sections outlined in double running stitch and filled with extremely complex geometric patterns. The original thread was waxed black silk and although other colours were sometimes used – occasionally red or gold-wrapped – they were seldom used together. Blackwork fell out of fashion for clothing but persisted on samplers. Nowadays, blackwork often incorporates one or two secondary colours.

THE HISTORY OF SAMPLERS

The word 'sampler' is derived from the French 'examplaire' meaning a model to be copied. Samplers were the forerunners of printed patterns, collections of stitches and motifs for sewing on to household linens and clothes. The earliest reference is recorded in 1502 on a bill of accounts for Elizabeth of York, wife of the English king Henry VII: 'for an elne (*sic*) of lynnyn cloth for a sampler for the Quene'. An ell measured 115 cm or 45 in.

Early English samplers were sewn on narrow linen strips, about 15–23 cm [6–9 in] wide cut across the width of the loom on which they were woven. Cloth was very expensive and designs were worked into every spare fibre. They displayed a huge variety of stitches in as many as twenty different colours of silk and metal threads.

Germany produced the first printed pattern book in 1523 and by the end of the century every other European country had followed suit. The oldest surviving sampler was signed and dated by Jane Bostocke of England in 1598 and certainly shows the influence of such patterns.

During the next century it became fashionable to add a border of geometric or floral design and from about 1650 moral inscriptions were included. The idea of the sampler as an educational tool had arrived and it then became a record of virtue and achievement.

Throughout the 1700s, samplers changed to a square format and into highly ornamental pictures, maps, and even mathematical tables, all of which were intended to show off the needleworker's skill in the craft.

By the end of the nineteenth century and the close of the Victorian era, the craze for the needlework motto had taken over. Pre-printed on perforated paper and sold for pennies, it usually featured a domestic or rural scene and a proverb or quotation from the Bible. Cross stitch was the dominant stitch and schoolchildren and hobbyists everywhere could produce very satisfying results.

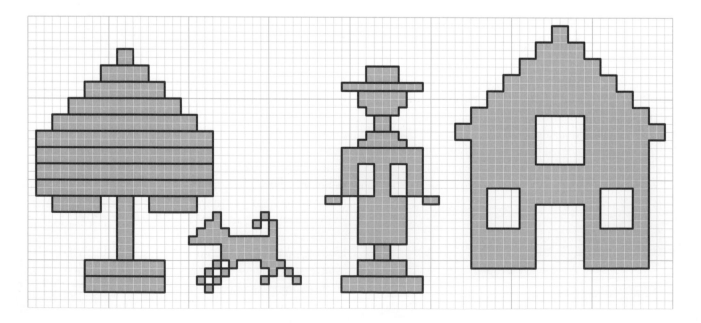

Four traditional sampler motifs: a tree, a dog, a man and a house.

BACKSTITCH ALPHABET

A sampler-style alphabet with matching numerals, designed to be executed in backstitch using just two strands of embroidery cotton [floss]. This alphabet is also suitable for lettering tiny keepsake items or for signing and dating your own work.

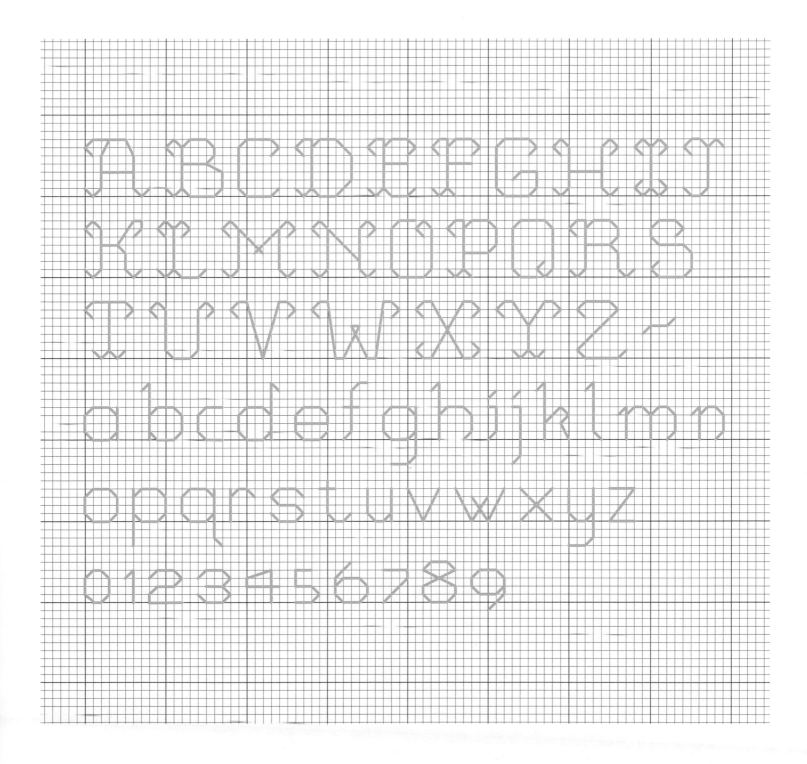

POPULAR SAMPLER MOTIFS

This page contains 15 popular motifs on a standard 10x10 grid for easy counting. Those with a backstitch outline can be worked without one, if you wish. Stitch them in one single colour or many, the choice is yours. And you can make them singly or combine them into pictures.

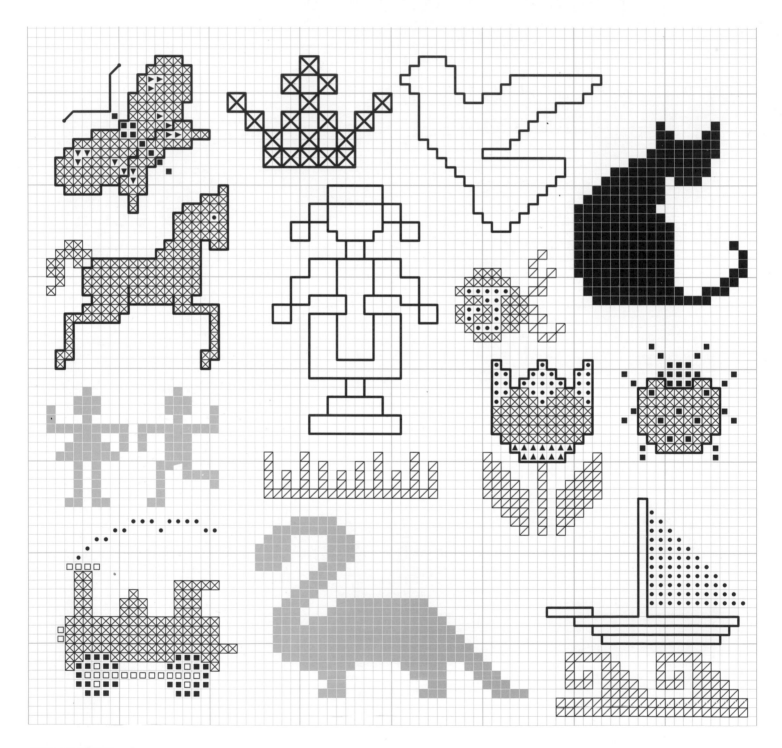

ASSISI WORK

Assisi work is a thirteenth-century embroidery technique from the Italian town of the same name. It consists of a 'voided' (ie blank) motif, outlined in backstitch or Holbein stitch, and surrounded by a background of solid cross stitch (for a range of cross stitch variations, see pp. 128–129).

Originally, nuns embroidered these designs on church altar cloths, working on plain linen in two colours of silk thread. The outline was usually stitched in black, with red or blue for the background filling; later, brown, green and gold were introduced.

Formal subjects suit Assisi work best, like heraldic beasts and mythical creatures. Traditionally, the creatures were arranged in symmetrical pairs between intricate borders worked in the same colour as the background.

To embroider a reproduction version, you will need a high-count cream linen evenweave (28-count or higher). You could dip it briefly in weak black tea to give it an antique look. Do not wring it; let it drip dry naturally and press before use. Experiment with the number of strands of thread to produce the effect you want but keep to the traditional colours. If you are using an 'antiqued' fabric, you will probably find softer shades look more authentic.

Of course, you can take the Assisi style and give it a more contemporary treatment with variegated threads or coloured evenweave fabric, and the motifs don't have to be traditional either.

HERALDIC BEASTS AND MYTHICAL CREATURES

A page of fantastic creatures set on a standard 10x10 grid. These are easily adapted for Assisi-style projects by 'voiding' the patterned squares, outlining them in Holbein stitch, and cross stitching the background instead. For the characteristic filigree borders found on Assisi work, see the example on the previous page or turn to p. 138.

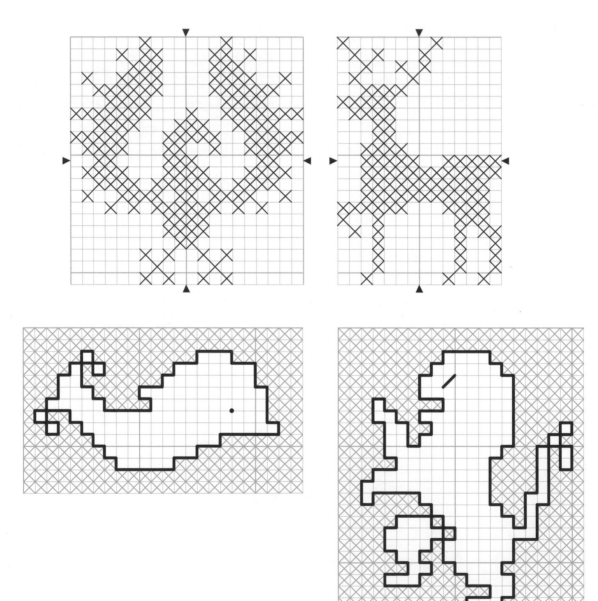

ASSISI-STYLE ALPHABET

These decorative initials are in marked contrast to the backstitch alphabet on p. 123.
The letters may be voided from the background, like Assisi work.

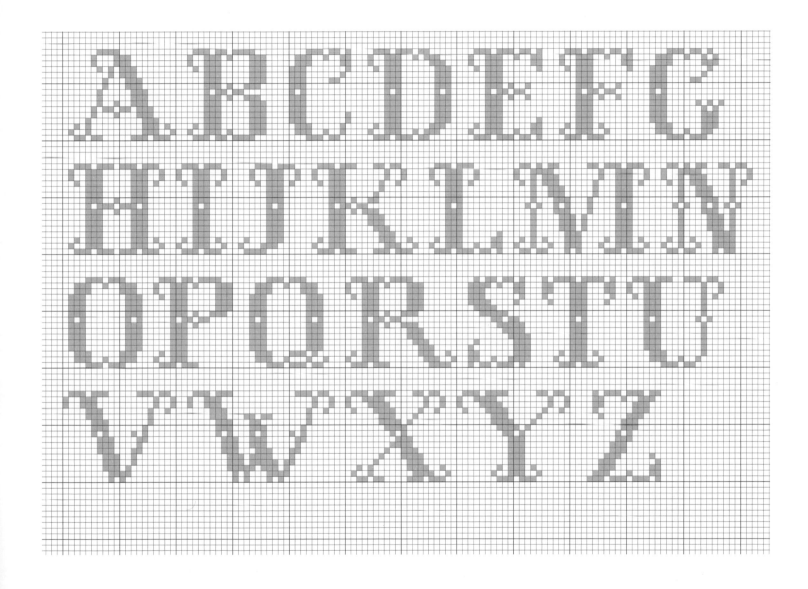

CROSS STITCH VARIATIONS

These diagrams show examples worked on evenweave fabric. For aida, halve the number of threads in the instructions and substitute squares. All of these stitches can be worked larger or smaller by increasing or decreasing the number of threads or squares that you work over.

Herringbone stitch

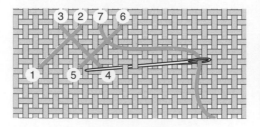

Stitch a diagonal 4 threads right and 4 threads up. Needle in at top and out 2 threads left. Stitch diagonal 4 threads right and 4 threads down. Needle in at base and out 2 threads left. Repeat to form a row, following the numbered points.

Threaded herringbone stitch

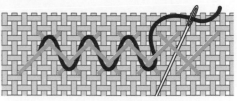

Work a row of herringbone stitch. Secure second colour thread on wrong side by whipping round existing stitches. Bring needle through and weave in and out of herringbone without stitching into fabric. Needle in and fasten off on wrong side.

Long-armed cross stitch

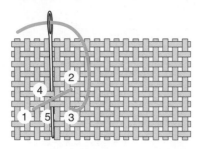

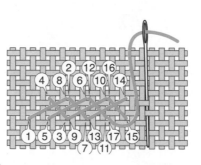

1 Following the numbers, stitch a long diagonal right. Needle in at top and out again below. Cross over previous stitch. Once again, needle in at top and out below.

2 Repeat to form a row, following the numbered points. Repeated rows make a bold background filling, especially for Assisi work.

Tied cross stitch

Work a cross stitch over 4 threads. Bring needle through, level with centre. Stitch across over 2 threads. Work a foundation row of cross stitch, then stitch central ties with a row of running stitch in a second colour.

Algerian eye stitch

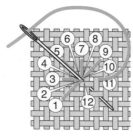

1 Bring needle through at left base and work 8 straight stitches clockwise into the same central hole, following the numbered points.

2 Pull stitches firmly to create the central hole. Do not allow threads on wrong side to cover it.

Smyrna (double cross) stitch

Bring needle through at left base. Stitch a diagonal 4 threads right and 4 threads up. Needle in at top and out 4 threads directly below. Work 3 more straight stitches, each over 4 threads, as numbered.

Boxed cross stitch

Work a vertical cross stitch over 4 threads. Box in with a square formation of 8 backstitch or Holbein stitches over 2 threads each.

Open filling stitch

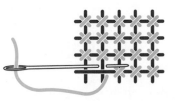

Work a grid of long, evenly spaced straight stitches. Bring needle through at each intersection and work a cross stitch over 2 or 3 threads. The cross ties can be a second colour. This is a good filler for blackwork.

Woven (braided) cross

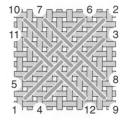

Bring needle through at left base. Stitch a diagonal 8 threads right and 8 threads up. Needle in at top and out 2 threads directly below. Work 3 more straight stitches, as numbered, before weaving the final 3 stitches in and out of the first set.

Tied half Rhodes stitch

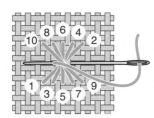

1 Bring needle through at left base. Stitch a diagonal 4 threads right and 4 threads up. Needle in at top and out 1 thread further right along base. Work 2 more straight stitches, following the numbered points, ending with a vertical.

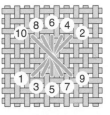

2 Stitch 2 more diagonals across the vertical, following the numbered points.

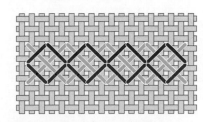

3 Bring needle through, level with centre point. Stitch across over 2 threads.

Rice stitch

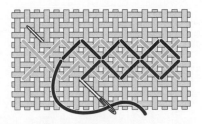

1 Bring needle through at base. Stitch a diagonal 4 threads right and 4 threads up. Needle in at top and out 4 threads directly below. Repeat to form a row, then return, completing the crosses.

2 In a second colour, backstitch over each half leg of each cross stitch. The backstitches are worked over 2 threads.

3 Rice stitch forms an effective background for contemporary Assisi work.

'Sans' is French for 'without', and letters without serifs do not have the little bracket-like features found at the ends of vertical and horizontal strokes in a serif alphabet (see opposite).

SERIF ALPHABET PLUS NUMERALS

KNOT STITCHES

Knots are indicated on charts by filled-in dots. The knot family plays a significant part in counted cross stitch, being ideal for tiny details on flowers and faces. However, people often have more trouble with these small stitches than any others. They need practice, no doubt, but it is also vital to use the correct needle. Tapestry needles have 'fat' eyes that do not make good coils; a fine, smooth, sharp embroidery needle is best.

French knot

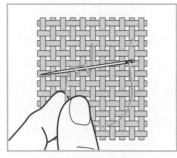 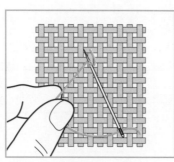 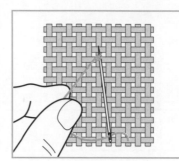 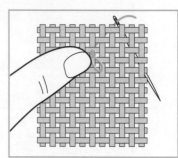

1 Wrap the thread around the needle as many times as the pattern requires.

2 Holding the needle in one hand, pull the thread gently until the coils tighten and start sliding down towards the tip.

3 Insert the needle close to where the thread originally came out. On evenweave, the distance is one thread; on aida, the next square. Avoid using the same hole or the knot will disappear to the wrong side.

4 With a firm grasp on the fabric, press down with your thumb to hold the coils in place and pull the needle and thread gently but firmly through to the other side, leaving a perfect knot on the surface.

Four-legged knot

This knot can be used singly or as a filling stitch. It looks good either upright or on the diagonal.

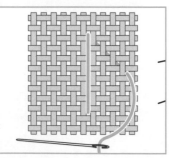 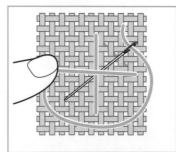 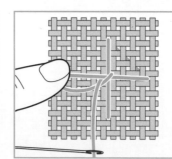

1 Make a vertical stitch over 8 threads. Needle in at top and out 4 threads below and 4 threads right, ready for the arms of the cross.

2 Hold thread across the mid-vertical with your thumb while sliding the needle diagonally from top right to base left. The looped thread hangs below the vertical stitch.

3 Pull needle and thread down carefully through the loop to form a knot and tighten it around the centre of the vertical.

4 Needle in 4 threads left, level with knot, to complete the cross.

PART THREE:
STITCHABLES

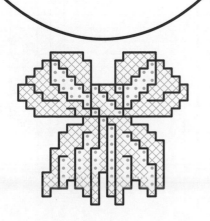

TEMPLATES

Stitchables include 'readymades' (see p. 114) and any items that you may have made yourself – like an apron, bag or cushion – or bought specially to embroider, such as a baby's bib, table runner or pillow cases.

Trace, copy or scan these templates for use as stitched borders, picture mounts or framed greetings cards. Cut them out carefully from paper or card with small pointed scissors or a craft knife (always cut away from your other hand, never towards it).

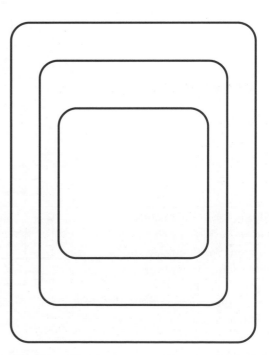

GREETINGS CARDS

Important occasions deserve to be marked with cards that people will treasure. Even for regular events like birthdays and New Year, hand-embroidered greetings send a special message.

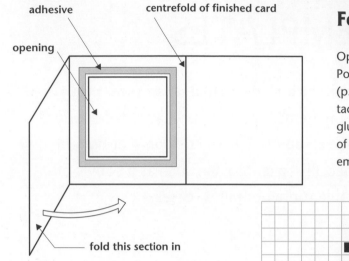

adhesive

centrefold of finished card

opening

fold this section in

Folded card mounts

Open the prepared card and place it face down on a clean sheet of paper. Position your work over the opening, using the tacking [basting] guidelines (p. 117) to centre it. Trim fabric margins to fit inside the card and remove tacking [basting]. Prepare the adhesive area with double-sided tape or fabric glue. Reposition the embroidery. If required, add tape or glue to the edges of the left-hand section before folding it over to conceal the back of the embroidery. Press down firmly.

A light box is not only handy for tracing designs; use it to position your work quickly and accurately when mounting and framing. No light box? If you have a glass-topped table, simply stand a lamp underneath it and your work surface is transformed.

DECORATIVE BANDS

Both evenweave and aida are available in narrow bands with pre-stitched edges, and in a growing range of colours.

Measuring 3.5–12 cm [1½–4 ¾ in] wide, these bands can be made into a variety of things, from curtain ties and cake bands to belts and small purses. Turn the raw ends over and line the finished work with broad ribbon, ironed onto the back with fusible web. For a firmer edge, the band and ribbon may be satin-stitched together by hand or machine.

Bookmarks

Create a classic bookmark with decorative initials using the alphabet below or on p. 127. First, tack [baste] your guidelines (p. 117), remembering to allow for turnings both ends. For a pointed end, fold the corners up to meet centre back in a triangle. Slip stitch together before pressing the lining into place. Finally, sew a tassel (p. 137) to the point.

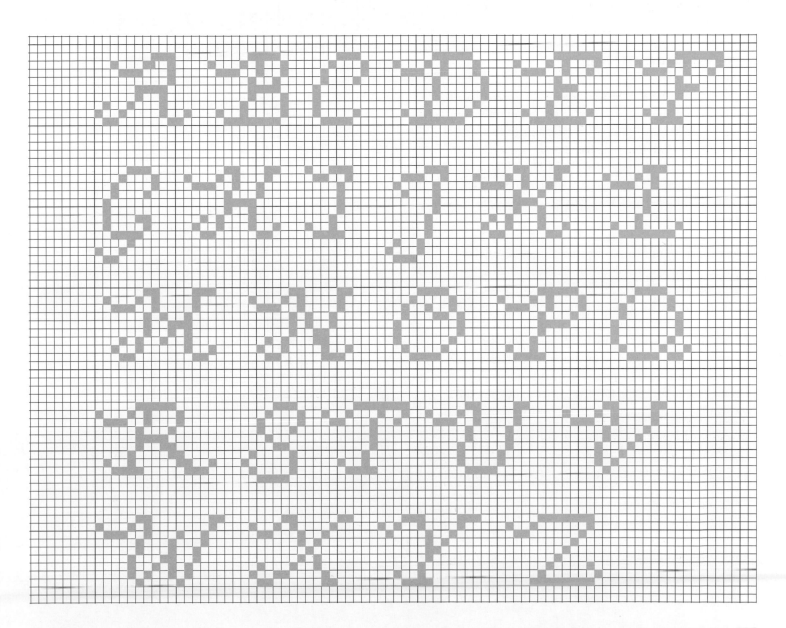

WORKING WITH PLASTIC CANVAS

Plastic canvas is ideal for three-dimensional projects because it is easy to cut to shape, ready to stitch. All you need is a sharp pair of scissors and some bright ideas.

The canvas (p. 109) is produced in various colours and 'clear'. Unless a background colour is part of your design, use the clear plastic. It comes in three forms: standard, rigid and soft. The rigid is good for stand-alone objects like frames and boxes, while the soft makes flexible items such as bangles and bag handles. Of the four mesh sizes, 7-count is the most popular, often worked with double knitting wool (worsted). Alternatively, use thick perle [pearl] cotton or 12 strands of embroidery cotton [floss] with a 16 or 18 needle.

Festive decorations

Draft the shapes onto standard canvas with a water-soluble marker. Cut the mesh and trim off the nubs; mistakes can be mended with superglue. Wash the shape to remove the ink before stitching. Combine blending filament (see rear cover photograph) with the main thread for a shimmering effect, or use lurex yarn. When you finally blanket-stitch (p. 141) round the edges, add glass beads for extra sparkle.

Make hangers from narrow ribbon or twist your own cord (right). Cut two lengths of rayon or metallic embroidery thread, four times as long as the desired cord. Knot together at both ends and ask someone to hold one end while you slot a pencil through the other. Pull the loop taut between you and start twisting. When you've done enough, the cord will curl up as you relax the tension. Place your finger halfway, release one end and allow it to twist on itself to make the full cord. Smooth out any kinks between thumb and forefinger. Secure with a knot.

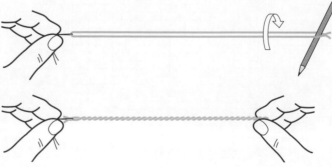

MINIATURE DESIGNS

Small-scale embroidery will fit many of the readymade items available from craft suppliers and is a good way of utilizing scraps of fabric and embroidery threads.

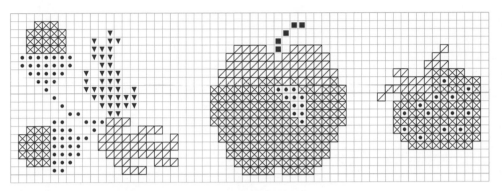

Trinket pots, pendants and fobs

Stitch your miniatures on 16- to 22-count aida, with two strands in a 26 or 28 needle. Readymades usually carry a card insert; draw crosslines on it like the guidelines on your work (p. 117). Align centres by sticking a pin through both, then draw lightly around the card. Cut the fabric out along the line and remove the tacking. Iron the embroidery face down, place inside the item, and seal.

Scissor keeper

Embroider two 65 mm [2 ½ in] squares of aida and press face down. Put right sides together and backstitch (p. 121) around three sides, with a 6 mm [¼ in] seam allowance. Clip the corners and turn right sides out. Stuff the cushion with some wadding and, before closing with blanket stitch (p. 141), insert both ends of a 40 cm [16 in] length of cord at one corner. Blanket stitch around all four sides. Make a tassel (see below) and sew it to the corner diagonally opposite the cord. Finally, loop the cord through one scissor handle.

Tassels

 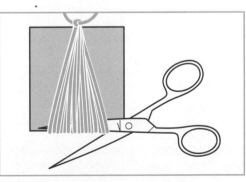 

1 Wrap the thread around the card. Thread one strand, 30 cm [12 in] long, under the top loops.

2 Tie this strand tightly at the top; the ends can be knotted or twisted later, or threaded up for sewing. Cut all the tassel loops free at the lower edge.

3 Take another length of thread and wind firmly round the loose strands to form the tassel head. Finish with a secure knot. Thread the ends into a needle and work neatly into the centre of the tassel before trimming level.

BORDERS AND CORNERS

An essential feature of samplers and Assisi work, borders are worked once the main design is complete. Clever use of colour can create a three-dimensional effect. Only one or two strands of thread are required for a fine-line backstitch border.

PART FOUR:
BASIC EMBROIDERY STITCHES

This section provides a taster for other hand embroidery stitches not generally linked with the counted thread technique. It features some of the simplest and most popular stitches used all over the world.

History and geography have played their part in the art of embroidery. For centuries wherever people have spun cotton, linen, silk or wool, embroidery of one kind or another has flourished; and wherever they have travelled, the stitches have been copied and adapted.

The design on this page was produced as an iron-on transfer in the 1950s but it has its origins in the crewel embroidery of the English Jacobean period, which had been influenced by oriental styles and, in turn, travelled on westward to America with the early settlers.

Decorated running stitch

Even a row of plain running stitch can look interesting when laced or whipped with a second colour. Secure the thread to existing stitches on the wrong side and bring the needle through.

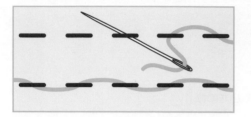

1 Lace by sliding the needle alternately up and down through the stitches without piercing the fabric until the end, when you fasten off on the wrong side.

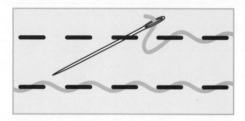

2 Whip by sliding the needle through each stitch from top to bottom only, without piercing the fabric until the end, when you fasten off on the wrong side.

Satin stitch

Satin stitch most probably originated in China, designed to show off the beautiful silk threads produced there. Work the stitches very closely together to cover the fabric completely. Needle in and out at the same angle and keep to a sharply defined outline.

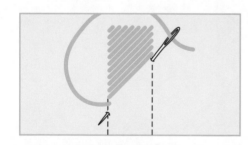

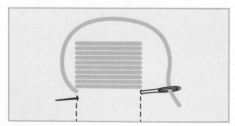

Stem stitch

This useful stitch is a variation on the backstitch and can follow curves or straight lines.

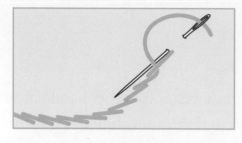

1 Work slanted backstitches with the needle coming out a little above the previous stitch.

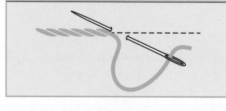

2 Create a thicker, more rope-like effect by inserting the needle at a sharper angle and increasing the number of strands to your thread.

Chain stitch

A looped stitch that is perfect for outlining and filling. It constructs well with three or more strands of embroidery cotton [floss].

1 Bring the needle through and push in again beside the exit hole. Leave a loop on the right side and bring the needle up through it at a short distance below the starting point. Pull gently until you have formed a rounded link in the chain.

2 Thread your needle with two colours and work alternate chain stitches with them. Take care to keep the unused thread *above* the needle point.

Daisy (Lazy Daisy) stitch

A favourite stitch for depicting flowers and leaves, this variation on the chain loop can be made to form a circle of as many petals as you wish.

 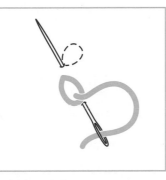

1 Begin as for chain stitch but work only one loop.

2 Instead of another link, make a very small tying stitch to hold the loop at its widest point. Bring the needle through again at the start of the next petal.

Buttonhole stitch

A relative of blanket stitch with the same basic construction. As the name suggests, this stitch evolved to seal the raw edges of a buttonhole and prevent the button rubbing the fabric. Stitched closely like satin stitch, it can be used to neaten both straight and curved edges and features in cutwork embroidery like broderie anglaise.

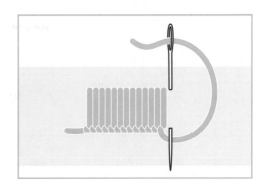

Blanket stitch

You might think this stitch belongs to domestic sewing rather than embroidery and it did indeed originate for the practical purpose of hemming blankets and towels. Nowadays it is more likely to be used purely decoratively.

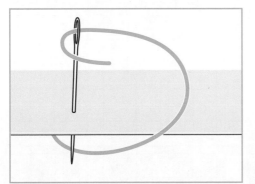  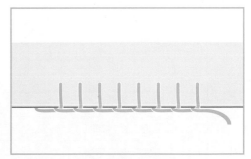

1 Secure the thread on the wrong side and bring it through at the folded edge of your fabric. Needle in at the desired stitch height and about 1 cm [³⁄₈ in] to the right, and out again directly below.

2 Pass the needle forwards through the loop, forming a half-hitch, and tighten the thread against the fold.

3 Repeat to form a row and fasten off with an extra half-hitch around the final loop before running the end into the fabric fold.

A script alphabet imitates handwriting. This one can be used both for
cross-stitch and as an outline for free embroidery in stem or chain stitch.

WASHING, MOUNTING AND AFTERCARE

Washing embroidery

However carefully you keep your work and hands clean, there are times when a completed embroidery needs freshening up. You may have an old family heirloom that you would like to clean or a second-hand item discovered in a charity shop.

Most contemporary embroidery threads are colourfast, but older ones may not be and hand-dyed threads will certainly run. Dark colours and all shades of red are the colours to be most wary of. If you have any doubts, make a test before plunging the entire piece into the wash. You can either soak short lengths of thread in hot water for a few minutes, or press a damp cotton wool pad against the stitching (preferably on the wrong side). If it runs, or stains the cotton wool, the embroidery must be dry cleaned.

If your piece is marked with wine, ink, grease or rust, there are several proprietary stain removers you could try before laundering; always follow the manufacturer's instructions on these products.

Embroidery should be hand washed in lukewarm water only. Use pure soap flakes or a liquid detergent suitable for delicates. Remove dirt by gently pressing and squeezing; do not rub the stitching. Rinse in several changes of cool water before rolling the embroidery in a clean towel to remove excess water. Unwrap and gently pull the piece into shape.

Spread another (dry) towel over a work surface or airing rack and lay the item out flat so moisture evaporates evenly from the surface. Do not dry by direct heat or in strong sunlight.

If the piece has become distorted and will not dry square, 'block' it by stretching and pinning on to a soft board (like foam board) using long, rustproof pins at frequent intervals all round the edge. Leave until totally dry.

Pressing

Embroidery is always ironed *face down* on a clean padded surface, and usually with a pressing cloth between the back of the work and the iron. This prevents the stitching from being flattened and losing its texture. Check that the heat setting is correct for the fabric. If you are not using a steam iron, dampen the pressing cloth to cope with any heavy creases.

Steam treatment helps to smooth out fabric that has been worked in a hoop. Hold the iron above the embroidery, passing it to and fro until the piece is evenly damp; then pull the fabric gently into shape, eliminating the bulge made by the hoop. Lay the embroidery face down again and – without a pressing cloth, so you can see what you're doing – press by setting the iron down and lifting straight up; don't drag it across the damp fabric. Allow the embroidery to cool where it lies.

Mounting

Although you may not want to make the frame yourself, mounting your own work is easy enough. Cut a mount from thin hardboard, mounting or foam board. Conservation board is an acid-neutral alternative. Hardboard needs to be sawn and your supplier should do this. For ordinary card or foam board, use a sharp craft knife (blunt blades are actually more dangerous) together with a metal straight edge and a cutting mat. Keep your fingers behind the cutting edge.

Some people like to pad their work for display. Cut the wadding [batting] to the exact size of the mount board. When using hardboard, you will mount the fabric against the rough side.

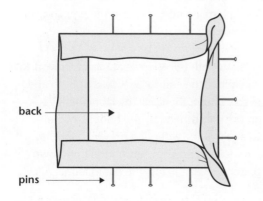

back

pins

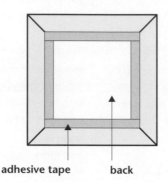

adhesive tape   back

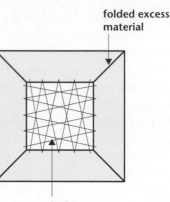

folded excess material

lacing

1 Lay the embroidery face down and place the mount board on top with the wadding [batting] in between. Fold the fabric up and pin into the edges of the board using glass-headed pins. Turn and check for positioning (you may need to re-pin a few times). Ensure the edges of the board align with the weave of the fabric.

2 Hardboard will not take pins, so use adhesive tape for positioning. If you don't want any lacing, fold the corners neatly, pull the fabric taut and tape the fabric fold-over to the back of the board all round. Be aware that adhesive tape eventually turns brittle and leaves sticky deposits; it should never be used on or near the embroidered area.

3 Fold the fabric corners neatly and start lacing across the back from the middle of one of the shorter sides. Use a strong thread and work a giant herringbone stitch (p. 128) from side to side to avoid straining on a single hole in the fabric. Keep the thread tight enough to pull the surface taut without distorting the embroidery. Repeat across the two remaining sides.

Aftercare

As with every other textile, the chief enemies of embroidered fabrics are dirt, damp and insect pests. If the piece is displayed without glass, it will need dusting. Dust builds up quickly and can absorb moisture, leading to mould. Careful use of a vacuum cleaner with adjustable suction is best. Cover the end of the cleaner hose with a nylon stocking and put the nozzle close but not touching. Fine detail can be brushed off with a clean, soft artist's brush.

If the piece is in storage, check regularly for moth. Shake it out and refold a different way; this also prevents permanent creases from setting in. Long-term storage requires that the item is put away clean, unstarched (silverfish love starch), interleaved and wrapped with acid-free white tissue paper. Do not store fabrics in poorly ventilated, damp or humid surroundings such as lofts, cellars and seldom-opened cupboards or chests.

TERMS AND ABBREVIATIONS

Aida Block weave fabric with regular construction and visible stitch holes

Algerian eye Cross stitch variation

Alphabets Charted letters and numerals for samplers and monograms

Anti-fray Liquid or spray to prevent fraying of cut edges

Assisi Thirteenth-century embroidery technique from the Italian town of the same name

Away waste knot Starting knot placed well away from the stitching area and later cut off

Backstitch Used to outline or define cross-stitched areas

Band Narrow strip of evenweave fabric with decorative trim

Batting [Wadding] Material used to pad mounted fabric

Binca Low-count (large scale) evenweave for use by children

Blackwork Decorative stitching, originally in black silk, brought to England from Spain in the Tudor period

Blending filament Fine metallic thread for combination with ordinary stranded cotton [floss]

Blocking Stretching and pinning fabric to shape

Bodkin Large blunt-tipped needle for threading ribbon and cord

Border Decorative frame stitched around a design

Braided (woven) cross Cross stitch variation

Buttonhole stitch Neatens both straight and curved edges and features in cutwork embroidery

Chart Detailed guide to stitch placement in counted-thread embroidery, usually in the form of a grid or graph

Count Number of threads per 2.5 cm [1 in] in a foundation fabric

Counted-thread embroidery Technique of decorative stitching over a predetermined number of threads in the foundation fabric

Double cross (Smyrna) stitch Cross stitch variation

Double running (Holbein) stitch Used in blackwork and Assisi work, constructed from two passes of running stitch

Duo canvas Double thread mesh, also called Penelope

Embroidery canvas Starched woven cotton or linen mesh in four count sizes

Embroidery frame Rectangular frame to keep embroidery taut while working

Embroidery hoop Frame of concentric hoops to keep embroidery taut

Evenweave Linen or cotton fabric with the same number of identical threads per inch (2.5 cm) counted vertically and horizontally

Flower thread Unmercerized cotton twist, non-divisible, with a matt finish

Fractional stitches Quarter, half and three-quarter cross stitches

Free embroidery A form of surface embroidery not regulated by counted threads

French knot Embroidery stitch used for small details

Grid The basis of a chart or pattern, each square representing one stitch

HPI Holes Per Inch

Herringbone stitch Cross stitch variation

Holbein (Double running) stitch Used in blackwork and Assisi work, constructed from two passes of running stitch

In the hand To hold fabric in the hand while stitching, not in a hoop or frame, enabling the stitcher to sew rather than stab

Key List of symbols and associated colours on cross stitch charts

Lark's head knot (Loop start) Technique for securing thread at the start of work

Laying tool Small pointed stick of metal or wood for smoothing threads

Linen High-count woven fabric with threads of irregular thickness, made from flax

Long armed cross stitch Cross stitch variation

Loop start (Lark's head knot) Technique for securing thread at the start of work

Making up Stretching and mounting finished work

Mercerized cotton Thread treated with sodium hydroxide to strengthen, add lustre and make easier to dye

Metallics Threads incorporating metal and textile fibres

Mono canvas Single thread mesh

Motif One single design element

Open filling stitch Cross stitch variation

Perforated paper Thin card perforated with holes in a grid formation in imitation of Victorian-style stitched cards and mottos

Perle [Pearl] Shiny 2-ply twisted thread, non-divisible

Plastic canvas Plastic perforated to form a rigid mesh and available in pre-cut shapes

Railroading Technique of separating and smoothing strands of thread while stitching

Rice stitch Cross stitch variation

S-twist Threads spun anti-clockwise

Sampler Decorative means of displaying a variety of embroidery stitches

Skein Length of embroidery cotton [floss] held together by paper tubes, trademarked and colour coded for reference

Smyrna (double cross) stitch Cross stitch variation

Space-dyed Different colours or shades, factory dyed at regular intervals along the thread

Stab method Used with a hoop or frame: stab the needle into the fabric and pull it through from the other side

Stranded Cotton or rayon threads [floss] consisting of divisible strands

Tacking [basting] Preliminary stitching, removed when work is finished

Threaded herringbone stitch Cross stitch variation

Tied cross stitch Cross stitch variation

Tweeding Different coloured strands threaded into the same needle, used for textural effect

Variegated Factory-dyed single colour ranging from light to dark at regular intervals along the thread

Vilene Non-woven interfacing, available plain or iron-on

Wadding [Batting] Material used to pad mounted fabric

WS Wrong side

Waste knot Starting knot placed on RS of fabric and later cut off

Woven (braided) cross Cross stitch variation

Z-twist Threads spun clockwise

KNITTING & CROCHET

Every generation rediscovers the satisfaction of making things by hand and there is particular pleasure to be had from creating unique clothes and accessories for your family or in knitting for a charity.

Knitting is one of the world's most popular crafts and not at all difficult to learn, together with its close relation, crochet. Both construct a fabric from interlocking loops of yarn rather than woven threads on a loom. The great advantage of knitting and crochet is that you can carry your work anywhere you go. And the fabric takes shape as you progress – no paper patterns or cutting out – all you have to do at the end is seam the pieces together.

Of course there are certain methods and techniques that a knitter needs to master before his or her creativity can really take flight. The basics of knitting are here, with step-by-step illustrations to guide you, plus sections on equipment, how to read printed patterns, four simple projects and a glossary. We also aim to be useful to those who first learned to knit as children and would like some quick revision in order to get started again. The terminology used is UK-standard, together with the relevant US terms alongside in square brackets [ ] to make this a practical guide for all readers.

Knitting is such an ancient craft that no one knows exactly when it began. It probably evolved during the Bronze Age from the knotting of fishing nets. A woman's hair net or snood, c.1400BCE, has been recovered from a peat bog in Denmark; and knitted split-toe socks have been found in Egyptian tombs. The craft clearly grew simultaneously in different parts of the world and no doubt sailors played their part in spreading the knowledge.

European knitting developed into a marketable skill, recognized by the setting up of professional knitting guilds. The only women admitted to these medieval guilds were widows who inherited their husbands' membership. It's interesting to note that knitting in the old days seems to have been a male occupation, while women were involved at the start of the process with carding and spinning the yarn fibres.

When the machinery of the Industrial Revolution replaced handworkers, hand knitting survived as a cottage industry and was the sole means of support for many poor families. During both World Wars people of all ages answered the call to Knit for Victory and produced thousands of socks, gloves, mufflers and sweaters for the troops. Whether for a livelihood, charity or leisure activity, knitting continues to provide clothes, toys and items for the home, and it all starts with one ball of yarn and a pair of knitting needles.

PART ONE:
EQUIPMENT AND MATERIALS

KNITTING NEEDLES CONVERSION CHART

METRIC	UK	USA
2.00 mm	14	0
2.25 mm	13	1
2.75 mm	12	2
3.00 mm	11	–
3.25 mm	10	3
3.50 mm	–	4
3.75 mm	9	5
4.00 mm	8	6
4.50 mm	7	7
5.00 mm	6	8
5.50 mm	5	9
6.00 mm	4	10
6.50 mm	3	10 .5
7.00 mm	2	–
7.50 mm	1	–
8.00 mm	0	11
9.00 mm	00	13
10.00 mm	000	15
12.00 mm	0000	17
16.00 mm	00000	19
19.00 mm	–	35
25.00 mm	–	50

CROCHET HOOKS CONVERSION CHART

METRIC	UK	USA
Steel		
1.00 mm	4	10
1.25 mm	3	8
1.50 mm	2.5	7
1.75 mm	2	6
2.00 mm	1	4
Aluminium or plastic		
2.00 mm	14	B–1
2.25 mm	13	B–1
2.75 mm	12	C–2
3.00 mm	11	C–2
3.25 mm	10	D–3
3.50 mm	9	E–4
3.75 mm	9	F–5
4.00 mm	8	G–6
4.50 mm	7	7
5.00 mm	6	H–8
5.50 mm	5	I–9
6.00 mm	4	J–10
6.50 mm	3	10.25
7.00 mm	2	K–10.5
8.00 mm	0	L–11
9.00 mm	00	M–13
10.0 mm	000	N–15
11.5 mm	–	P–16
16.0 mm	–	Q
19.0 mm	–	S

EQUIPMENT FOR KNITTING AND CROCHET

Both knitting and crochet use simple tools that cost relatively little, although it is always worth investing in the best you can afford.

Knitting needles (A), sometimes called pins or sticks, are made in aluminium, plastic, wood and bamboo. Fast knitters favour the ultra-smoothness of aluminium whereas total beginners will find plastic better because it is less slippery and grips the yarn. Wood and bamboo are materials both warm to the touch and quieter to work with.

Standard needles are sold in pairs, with a smooth point at one end and a knob at the other to prevent your stitches sliding off. A **circular needle (B)** is a flexible plastic tube with pointed metal ends, for knitting large items like blankets, or garments without seams. Sets of three or four **double-pointed needles (C)** are made for knitting gloves and socks in the round. Special **cable needles (D)**, in various shapes, hold the complex rope-like patterns of fishermen's jerseys.

A **needle gauge and combined ruler (E)** is a doubly useful thing. **Stitch holders (F)** can hold your stitches safe or keep colours separate. **Row counters (G)** and **coloured markers (H)** help to record

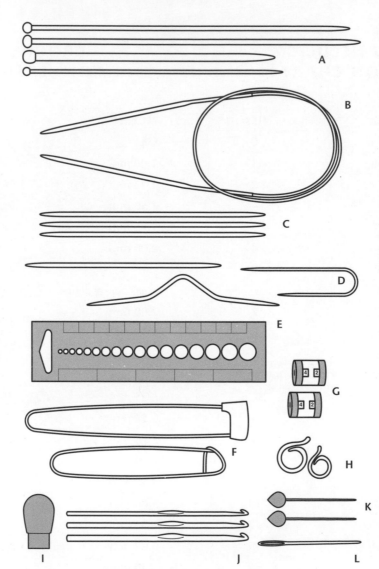

your progress, and **point protectors (I)** ensure that stitches stay on the needle when you store everything away.

Crochet hooks (J) are made in steel, aluminium, plastic, wood and bamboo. Steel ones are smooth, rigid, and machined to the smallest diameters for lacework with fine thread. Aluminium hooks are similar, and some have comfortable handles attached. Plastic hooks are lightweight and cheaper than metal but sometimes prove too flexible for tight work with a firm yarn. Crochet hooks are short, usually 13–15 cm [5–6 in] long, because – unlike knitting – crochet works with few stitches on the hook at once.

Useful items to both crafts are: **long pins (K)** for measuring tension samples (p. 151) and blocking (p. 168); and a range of **blunt-tipped yarn needles (L)** for sewing seams or embroidering without splitting the yarn.

Basic equipment: **Small sharp scissors** and a **fibreglass tape measure**.

YARNS AND FIBRES

The yarns for knitting and crochet are spun from a wide range of fibres, natural and man-made, often a blend of both. They are constructed in various ways too, giving us a choice of textures, from a basic 2- or 4-ply to velvety chenille or sparkling metallic.

Natural yarns include wool, mohair, angora and silk – all good for warmth – farmed from sheep, goats, rabbits and silkworms. Manufacturers also process plant fibres such as cotton, flax (linen) and bamboo, producing yarns that are cool and absorbent. Synthetic yarns like acrylic, polyester, nylon and viscose are popular for their hardwearing and easy-care properties.

It is important to choose the most suitable yarn for your purpose, so read the information on the ball bands carefully. You may want an item to be machine-washable or crease-resistant or a good candidate for felting (p. 189). And check the fibre content – some people are sensitive to wool and can only wear synthetics.

Fibres are first spun into single strands called *plys*. The separate plys are then twisted together to form a yarn. However, a single ply can be any thickness, so it does not signify a standard weight; in fact, a very thick yarn may contain fewer strands than a fine one.

Yarn is sold by weight not length. This is another reason to study the ball bands because length of yarn per ball is given there in yards and metres. This information could actually save you money, for instance, 50 gm of a lightweight wool goes further than 50 gm of a much heavier yarn like cotton.

Using thicker or thinner yarn, needles and hooks alters the size of the finished work. This table is a general guide only. Ball bands and printed patterns always recommend a combination of yarn weight and needle or hook size.

Experiment for fun by knitting with any pliable material: string, ribbon, raffia – even plastic bags cut into thin strips.

Buy enough yarn for the whole project. Check that the dye lot number is the same on all the ball bands.

100 gm 100% acrylic
294 metres / 322 yards

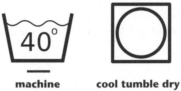

| machine washable | cool tumble dry | cool iron |

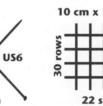

| may dry clean | 8UK US6 4 mm | 10 cm x 10 cm 30 rows 4 x 4 in 22 sts |

YARN, NEEDLE AND HOOK TABLE

UK	USA	NEEDLE SIZE	HOOK SIZE
2-ply	Lace / Light fingering	2.00 mm	1.25 mm
3-ply	Fingering	2.75 mm	1.25–2.50 mm
4-ply	Sport / Baby	3.25 mm	2.50–4.00 mm
Double knitting	Sport / Worsted	3.50–4.50 mm	4.00–6.00 mm
Aran	Fisherman / Medium	5.00–7.00 mm	6.00–8.00 mm
Chunky	Bulky	5.5–7.00 mm	8.00–10.00 mm
Super chunky	Super bulky	7.00–12.00 mm	9.00–16.00 mm

HOW TO READ KNITTING AND CROCHET PATTERNS

At the start of any project, take time to look over the printed pattern, including the section on making up the finished item. Working instructions are divided under separate headings ('Back', 'Front' etc), and it's generally best to make the pieces in the given order.

If you are using a printed pattern for the first time, don't be put off by all the abbreviations, brackets and stars. This is done to save space and it is a standard code that you will soon get used to.

Clothes patterns usually cover a range of sizes from smallest to largest, expressed like this:

To fit chest 66 [71 : 76 : 81.5] cm (26 [28 : 30 : 32] in).

Throughout the printed pattern you will see that the number of stitches and rows required for each size are laid out in the same way. It helps to highlight all the figures applicable to your size before you begin.

Decorative stitch combinations call for a specific number or *multiple* of stitches, so that the surface pattern fits exactly within the row or round. For instance, if the pattern calls for a multiple of 7 stitches plus 2 (1 extra stitch at either end for seam allowance), the total number of stitches should be a multiple of 7 (14, 21, 28, etc), plus 2.

A pair of brackets [ ] or ( ) will enclose a particular stitch combination and means that it must be repeated in the order shown. Here is a knitting example:

P2 (k2,p2) ten times, k3.

Meaning: After purling the first two stitches, repeat knitting two and purling two ten times (40 stitches in all), then knit the last three.

When a star or asterisk* is placed before an instruction, it means that the stitches following it must be repeated from that point. Here is an example from a round of crochet:

3ch, *2tr into next tr, 1tr; rep from * around, join with a ss into first ch.

Meaning: Chain three stitches, then crochet two trebles into the top of the next treble from the previous round, and one treble into the next; repeat the sequence of trebles right round to the first chain stitch, and join with a slip stitch.

You will find a complete list of abbreviations and terms for both knitting and crochet on pp. 190–191.

TENSION [GAUGE] SAMPLES FOR KNITTING AND CROCHET

The required stitch tension [gauge] appears on every knitting or crochet pattern. It is vital to the size of the finished work and matches the tension achieved by the designer of the original piece.

Tension [gauge] is written as the number of stitches and number of rows measured on a 10x10 cm [4x4 in] square created by working the pattern stitch in a specific needle or hook size.

For example:

20 sts and 22 rows to 10 cm [4 in] over st st on 5.50 mm needles

12 sts and 5 rows to 10 cm [4 in] in pattern on 6.50 mm crochet hook

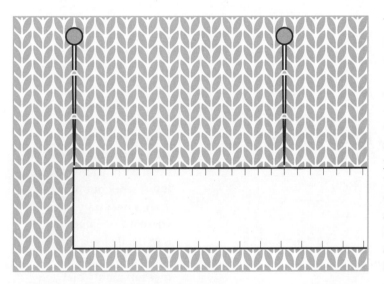

To do your own test, work an area slightly larger than 10x10 cm [4x4 in] square in the pattern stitch, using the stated yarn and needle – or hook – size. Pin your sample flat on a firm surface, *without stretching*. Measure a 10x10 cm [4x4 in] square in the centre with a ruler and mark it out with four long pins.

Count the rows and stitches between the pins; include half stitches or rows because these will add up on a large project. If your sample has too few stitches or rows to the square, then your tension is too loose and you should try again with smaller needles or hook. If there are too many stitches, it is too tight and you should try a larger size. Experiment until you reach the correct horizontal and vertical tension. If you must choose between achieving one but not the other, then go with the correct width; length is easily adjusted by working more or fewer rows.

> **Knitting that is too loose causes rubbing between stitches, which in turn causes the yarn fibres to break away and form unsightly little balls on the surface of the fabric, called pilling [bobbling or linting]. Various brushes, combs and shavers are available for removing it.**

CALCULATING QUANTITIES

If you want to change the type of yarn from the one specified in a printed pattern, first test its suitability with a tension [gauge] sample (p. 151). When you are satisfied with the tension, find a printed pattern for a similar style that uses your new yarn type, and take the suggested quantities as a guide.

Another way of calculating is to work through an entire ball of the new yarn, measure the area, then estimate the total area of your design and calculate how many balls it will take to complete it.

This method also applies if you want to calculate quantities for a change of stitch pattern rather than the yarn itself. Bear in mind, though, that any variation from a plain stitch to a fancy one will always consume more yarn.

How much you get from a ball depends on the qualities of the yarn fibre. If you substitute cotton or metallic yarn for wool, they have less elasticity and you will have to add stitches to compensate for a tighter fabric, and so it will take more yarn overall. Conversely, loosely twisted yarns go further, as do synthetics generally, so working the latter with a loose tension could result in a considerable saving.

ROUGH QUANTITIES FOR A LONG-SLEEVED SWEATER BASED ON WEIGHT AND FIBRE

(Allow about 30% less for sleeveless or children's garments)

YARN WEIGHT	100 gm BALLS	YARN FIBRE	100 gm BALLS
Medium	3–4	Acrylic and nylon	3–4
Double knitting	4–5	Acrylic and wool	4
Aran	6	Pure wool	5
Chunky	7	Cotton	6

A knitting and crochet yarn calculator is available as an iPhone application. It will work out how much yarn is necessary for a standard sweater, socks, hat, blanket etc, based on the tension [gauge] and measurements that you enter.

PART TWO:
KNITTING METHODS AND TECHNIQUES

HOLDING YARN AND NEEDLES

How you hold your knitting needles and yarn affects the evenness and tension of the fabric. There are no set rules, so try the methods shown until you find a way that suits you best. It may look complicated, but threading the working end of the yarn through your fingers not only makes knitting faster but controls the yarn better and produces a firm, even result.

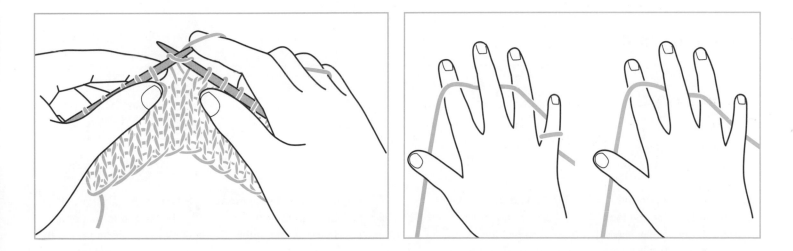

CASTING [BINDING] ON

Assembling the first row of stitches on the needle is known as casting [binding] on. Subsequent rows build on this initial row of loops. You can cast [bind] on using either two needles, or a single needle and your thumb.

Two needle method

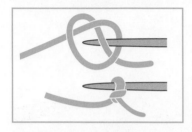  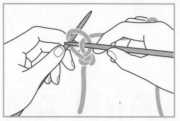 

1 Make a slip loop in the end of the yarn and tighten the loop around one needle, leaving a 15-cm [6-in] tail.

2 With this needle in your left hand, insert the tip of your right-hand needle into the loop from front to back. Wind the yarn under and over the tip of the right-hand needle.

3 Keep the new loop on the right-hand needle and the slip loop on the left. Slide the right-hand needle from behind the left, drawing the yarn through the slip loop to form a new stitch.

4 Insert your left-hand needle into the new stitch from front to back and withdraw the right one completely. Pull gently on the working yarn to tighten the new stitch around the left-hand needle.

Repeat until you have the required number of stitches on the left-hand needle (the initial loop counts as a stitch).

Thumb method

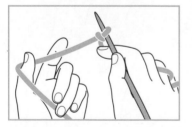  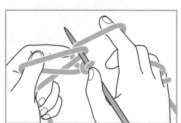 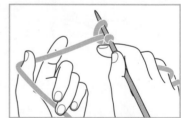

1 Make a slip loop in the yarn and tighten the loop around a single needle, leaving a tail of 250 cm [100 in], long enough to cast [bind] on 100 stitches. With the needle in your right hand, wrap the tail of yarn clockwise around the top joint of your left thumb.

2 Holding the tail down across your palm, insert the tip of the needle into the loop around your thumb.

3 Working with the yarn from the ball, wind the yarn under and over the tip of the needle.

4 Draw the yarn through the loop to form a new stitch and tighten it around the needle by gently pulling both working yarn and tail.

Repeat until you have the required number of stitches on the needle (the initial loop counts as a stitch).

CASTING [BINDING] OFF

When you have finished knitting, secure all the stitches by casting [binding] off so that they don't unravel. This same technique is used in decreasing, for example when shaping armholes (pp. 164–165). You can cast [bind] off on either a knit or purl row; see p. 156 for how to do knit or purl stitch. Keep the same tension as the rest of your work and try not to pull too tightly. Use the Lace cast [bind] off variation for a more stretchy result.

Casting [binding] off

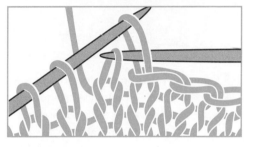

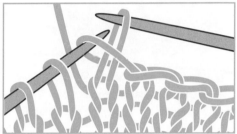

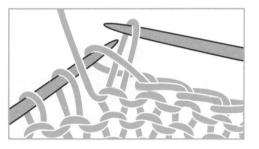

1 KNITWISE: Begin by knitting the first two stitches of your cast-off line and insert the tip of your left-hand needle into the first of the two.

2 KNITWISE: Lift the first stitch over the second and withdraw your left-hand needle so that the first stitch lies cast-off around the base of the second. One stitch remains on your right-hand needle; now knit the next stitch so that there are two again.

3 PURLWISE: Work the purl cast-off line in the same way but purl each stitch instead of knitting it.

Repeat until one stitch remains on the right-hand needle. Cut the yarn, leaving a tail of 15 cm [6 in]. Slide the final stitch off the needle, slip the yarn end through and pull gently until it lies flat with the rest of the row. Thread the tail into a blunt-tipped yarn needle and weave it into the selvedge [selvage] for about 7 cm [3 in].

The Lace cast [bind] off

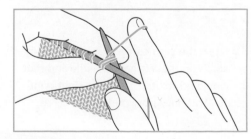

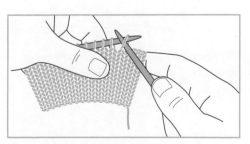

Repeat until one stitch remains on the right-hand needle. The purl version of this method is sometimes called the Russian cast [bind] off.

1 Knit together the first two stitches on the left needle, inserting the tip of your right-hand needle into the *back* of both loops.

2 Slip the new stitch you have made on the right needle back to the left needle, ready to knit it together with the next in line.

THE BASIC STITCHES AND MORE

Knit stitch and purl stitch are the two basic knitting stitches. Start both by holding the needle with the cast on stitches in your left hand, and the yarn and second needle in your right.

Knit stitch (k)

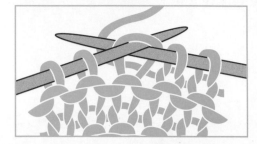 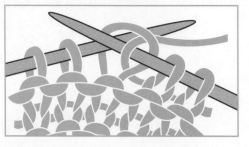 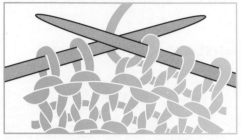

1 With the yarn at the back, insert the tip of your right-hand needle into the first stitch on your left-hand needle from front to back.

2 Wind the yarn under and over the tip of the right-hand needle. Form a new loop by sliding the tip of the right-hand needle up over the left.

3 Draw the yarn completely through the stitch on the left-hand needle and slide the whole new stitch on to the right-hand needle. You have now knitted one stitch.

Repeat this action into each stitch on the left-hand needle until they have all been worked on to the right-hand needle. You have now knitted a whole row. To knit the second row, change the needle holding all the stitches to your left hand and hold the empty needle in your right so that you are ready to work another row in the same way.

Purl stitch (p)

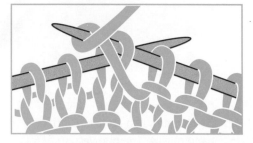 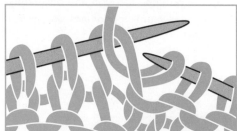 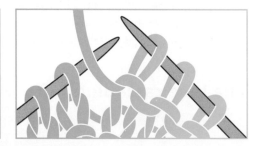

1 With the yarn at the front, insert the tip of your right-hand needle into the first stitch on your left-hand needle from back to front. Wind the yarn over and around the tip of the right-hand needle.

2 Form a new loop by sliding the tip of the right-hand needle down below the left.

3 Draw the yarn completely through the stitch on the left-hand needle and slide the whole new stitch on to the right-hand needle. You have now purled one stitch.

Repeat this action into each stitch on the left-hand needle until they have all been worked on to the right-hand needle. You have now purled a whole row. To purl the second row, change the needle holding all the stitches to your left hand and hold the empty needle in your right so that you are ready to work another row in the same way.

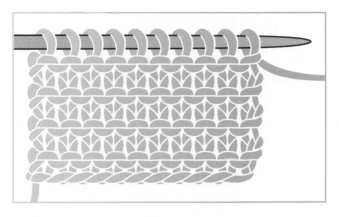

Garter stitch (g-st)

K every row.

The same effect is also achieved by working every row as purl (p).

Knitting cannot be easier than garter stitch, which works on any number of stitches.

PROJECT

If you are looking for your first project, try making a garter stitch scarf in double knitting or chunky wool on 6.00 mm [US 10] needles. Cast [bind] on 50–70 stitches and knit to the desired length before casting [binding] off. As a finishing touch, decorate the ends with a fringe (p. 171).

Stocking [stockinette] stitch (st st)

Row 1: K
Row 2: P
Repeat these two rows for pattern.

The 'right' side (RS) of the fabric will look like a series of smooth Vs (see p. 151), while the 'wrong' side (WS) looks like a series of horizontal ridges. Fabric made in stocking [stockinette] stitch tends to curl at the sides.

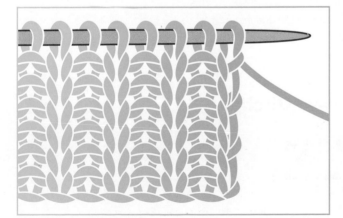

Single (1x1) rib

Multiple of 2 stitches
Every row *K1, p1; rep from * to end.

Be sure to purl the stitches that were knitted on the previous row and vice versa, otherwise the distinct vertical pattern will not be made. Ribbing produces a stretchy, flexible knit, ideal for collars, cuffs and waistbands.

Double (2x2) rib

Multiple of 4 stitches
Every row *K2, p2; rep from * to end.

Be sure to purl the stitches that were knitted on the previous row and vice versa, otherwise the distinct vertical pattern will not be made.

Moss [seed] stitch (m-st)

Multiple of 2 stitches
Row 1: *K1, p1; rep from * to end.
Row 2: *P1, k1; rep from * to end.
Repeat these two rows for pattern.

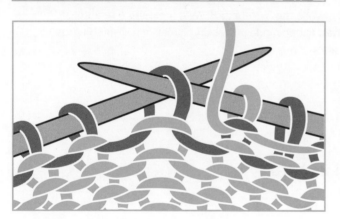

Slip stitch (sl)

Transfer a stitch from your left-hand needle to the right-hand needle without working the yarn. Unless otherwise instructed, always slip stitches purlwise, with the tip of the right-hand needle crossing in front of the left, as if preparing to do a purl stitch. This keeps the stitch untwisted and facing the same way as before.

Double moss [moss] stitch

See rear cover photograph 1

Multiple of 4 stitches plus 2
Row 1: K2, *p2, k2; rep from * to end.
Row 2: P2, *k2, p2; rep from * to end.
Row 3: as row 2.
Row 4: as row 1.
Repeat rows 1 to 4 for the pattern.

Basketweave stitch

See rear cover photograph 2

Multiple of 8 stitches plus 3
Row 1: (RS) K.
Row 2: K4, p3, *k5, p3; rep from * to last 4 sts, k4.
Row 3: P4, k3, *p5, k3; rep from * to last 4 sts, p4.
Row 4: as row 2.
Row 5: K.
Row 6: P3, *k5, p3; rep from * to end.
Row 7: K3, *p5, k3; rep from * to end.
Row 8: as row 6.
Repeat rows 1 to 8 for the pattern.

PROJECT: TODDLER'S RIBBED HAT WITH TURN-UP AND POMPOM

Multiples of 4 stitches

Use chunky wool on 6.00 mm [US 10] needles or two strands of double knitting yarn together (in different colours for a tweed effect).

This hat is intended for 1–3 year-olds, although double rib has great stretchability and it may fit a slightly older child. Results depend on your stitch tension as well as any variation you may choose in needle size or yarn thickness. Work a sample first (p. 151); cast on 20 st and knit 10 rows in k2, p2 rib. Unstretched, it should measure about 10 cm [4 in] wide.

Cast on 60 stitches.
Row 1: K tbl to end of row, for a neat edge.
Row 2: K to end of row.
Row 3: (RS) *K2, p2; rep from * to end of row.
Work for a total of 34 rows in k2 p2 rib pattern. Work measures 21.5 cm [8.5 in], including a turn-up of 5 cm [2 in].

Decreasing

Row 1: (RS)*K2, p2tog; rep from * to end of row (45 st rem).
Row 2: *K1, p2; rep from * to end of row.
Row 3: *K2tog, p1; rep from * to end of row (30 st rem).
Row 4: *K1, p1; rep from * to end of row.
Row 5: *K1, p1, k2tog; rep from * to last 2 st, k1, p1 (23 st rem).
Row 6: *P2tog; rep from * to last st, p1 (12 st rem).
Row 7: *K2tog; rep from * to end of row (6 st rem).

Cut yarn leaving a long tail of approx 90 cm [36 in]. Thread up a large tapestry or yarn needle. Carefully remove the 6 remaining stitches from the needle and, holding them firmly at their base, pull the needle and long yarn tail through the loops.

Draw the 6 st into a ring and secure with a back stitch before using the rest of the tail to seam the hat from crown to brim. Take care to keep the rib pattern straight down the join.

Make a 5.5 cm [2.25 in] pompom (p. 172) and sew to the top of the hat.

Eyelet cable

See rear cover photograph 3

An alternative stitch pattern for the more adventurous (average 8st = 2.5cm [1 in]), which works well for hats and scarves

Cast on multiples of 5 stitches plus 2
Row 1: (RS) P2, *k3, p2; rep from * to end.
Row 2: (WS) K2, *p3, k2; rep from * to end.
Row 3: P2, * sl 1 purlwise, k2, psso the k2, p2; rep from * to end.
Row 4: K2, *p1, yrn, p1, k2; rep from * to end.
Repeat rows 1 to 4 for the pattern.

AVERAGE HEAD CIRCUMFERENCE AND HAT HEIGHT

TODDLER 1–3 years	Circumference 46–51 cm [18–20 in]	Height 20 cm [8 in]
CHILD 3–10 years	Circumference 48–52 cm [19–20.5 in]	Height 21.5 cm [8.5 in]
YOUNG ADULT	Circumference 52–56 cm [20.5–22 in]	Height 23–26 cm [9–10 in]
WOMAN	Circumference: 54–57 cm [21.5–22.5 in]	
MAN	Circumference: 58.5–61 cm [23– 24 in]	

SELVEDGES [SELVAGES]

Edges not only look better when they are evenly knitted but also make seam sewing easier. One tip for tidy edges, especially when using stocking stitch, is to knit the first four stitches in every row tightly and the final four loosely; this way the selvedge [selvage] tension levels out each time you turn your work.

Slipped stitch selvedge [selvage]

On knit rows, slip the first stitch knitwise and knit the last stitch of the row.

On purl rows, slip the first stitch purlwise and purl the last stitch of the row.

This method neatens both edges and produces a little bump, appearing every second row. The bumps make counting rows easy and help when joining pieces and matching seams accurately.

Open selvedge [selvage]

On knit rows, slip the first and last stitches of every row knitwise.

Purl all the edge stitches in the purl row.

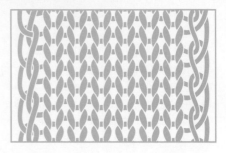

For use only when the edge of your work is to be left open, as on a scarf. It is too loose to withstand seaming to another piece.

ADDING NEW YARN WITHOUT KNOTTING

This is the way to add new yarn at the start of a row if you are knitting horizontal stripes.

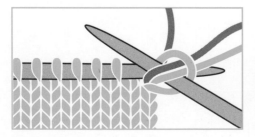

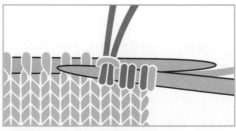

When you have finished, weave the loose ends into the edge or back of your work with a yarn needle.

1 Insert your right-hand needle into the first stitch on the left-hand needle and wrap both old and new yarns over it. Knit one stitch with both yarns together.

2 Drop the old yarn and knit the next two stitches with double thickness of the new yarn, then drop the tail of the new yarn and continue knitting in pattern. Treat the double stitches as normal when working the subsequent row.

EMERGENCY PROCEDURES

Picking up dropped stitches

The diagrams show how to pick up a dropped stitch on a *knitted* row.

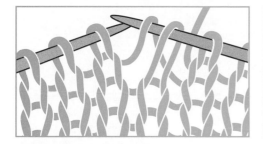 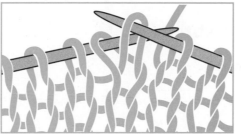 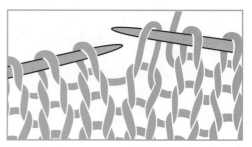

1 A dropped stitch on a knitted row appears with the missed strand behind it.

2 Insert the right-hand needle through the empty loop, catch the missed strand and pull it through on to the right-hand needle.

3 Transfer the rescued loop to the left-hand needle so it untwists to face the correct way and is ready to knit as usual.

Work in reverse for a purled row, where the missed strand lies in front of the dropped stitch.

Mending ladders

When a dropped stitch unravels downwards it forms a 'ladder'. Use a crochet hook to retrieve the stitch and climb back by pulling each successive 'rung' either forwards (knit) or backwards (purl) through the loop.

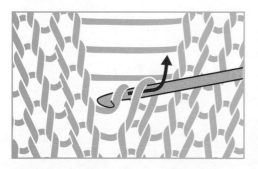 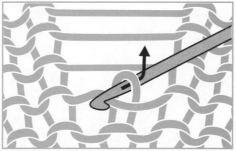

1 Mending a ladder on a knitted row.

2 Mending a ladder on a purled row.

Unpicking a mistake

If you make a mistake before you finish a row it is quite simple to unpick your stitches in order to correct the error.

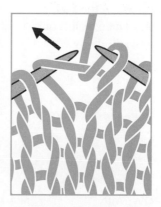

Insert the tip of your left-hand needle into the loop below the last stitch that you worked on the right-hand needle. Transfer this loop onto the left-hand needle allowing the stitch above it to slip off the right-hand needle. Repeat as far back as necessary.

INCREASING

When knitting a garment, it is necessary to shape the fabric and this means adding stitches. There are several methods of increasing.

Working twice into the same stitch (Inc 1)

This method is used to shape the edges of a piece.

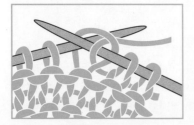 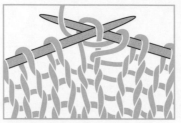  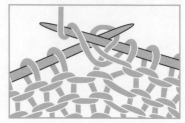

1 **KNITWISE:** With yarn at the back, insert the right-hand needle from front to back and knit a stitch in the usual way without sliding it off the left-hand needle.

2 **KNITWISE:** Keeping the new loop on the right-hand, insert the right-hand needle into the *back* of the same stitch on the left-hand one and knit again, completing the transfer to the right-hand needle.

3 **PURLWISE:** With yarn at the front, insert the right-hand needle from back to front and purl a stitch in the usual way without sliding it off the left-hand needle.

4 **PURLWISE:** Keeping the new loop on the right-hand, insert the right-hand needle into the *back* of the same stitch on the left-hand one and purl again, completing the transfer to the right-hand needle.

Raised increase between stitches (M1)

For tailored shaping within the body of a piece. This method is neater if worked on a knit row. It is quite hard to manipulate the right-hand needle on a purl row.

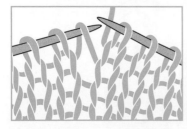 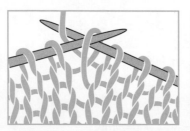 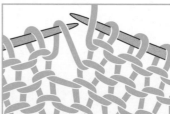 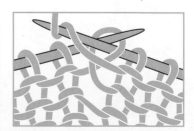

1 **IN A KNIT ROW:** With the tip of the left-hand needle inserted from front to back, raise the strand that runs between the stitches on your left- and right-hand needles.

2 **IN A KNIT ROW:** Knit into the *back* of the raised strand. This avoids creating a hole in the fabric. The new stitch ends on the right-hand needle.

3 **IN A PURL ROW:** With the tip of the left-hand needle inserted from front to back, raise the strand that runs between the stitches on your left- and right-hand needles.

4 **IN A PURL ROW:** Purl into the *back* of the raised strand. This avoids creating a hole in the fabric. The new stitch ends on the right-hand needle.

Lifted increase (K up 1 or p up 1)

This method suits paired increases, such as shaping raglan sleeves. It can tighten the fabric so you should work with a looser tension.

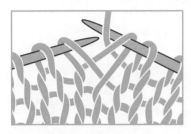 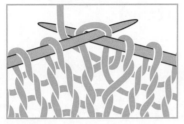 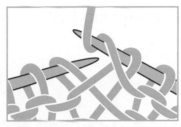 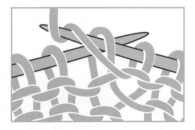

1 **KNITWISE:** Insert your right-hand needle from front to back into the top of the stitch below the next one to be knitted. Knit this in the usual way and create a new stitch.

2 **KNITWISE:** Then knit the next stitch on the left-hand needle.

3 **PURLWISE:** Insert your right-hand needle from back to front into the top of the stitch below the next one to be purled. Purl this in the usual way and create a new stitch.

4 **PURLWISE:** Then purl the next stitch on the left-hand needle.

Decorative increase (Yfwd, yrn or yo)

Used in lace and other decorative work, this method (also called the 'yarn-over') forms an openwork pattern, which can also be used to make buttonholes.

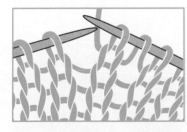 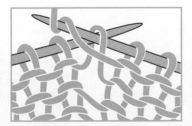 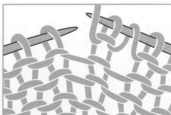 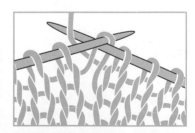

1 **KNITWISE (Yfwd /yo):** Bring yarn forward and loop over the right-hand needle. Knit the next stitch and finish the row.

2 **KNITWISE (Yfwd /yo):** On the next row, purl or knit the yarn-over loop in the usual way. Work in pattern to the end of the row.

3 **PURLWISE (Yrn):** Take yarn back over the right-hand needle and then under to the front of your work. Purl the next stitch and finish the row.

4 **PURLWISE (Yrn):** On the next row, knit or purl the yarn-over loop in the usual way. Work in pattern to the end of the row.

DECREASING

Like increasing, decreasing is also necessary to shape the fabric that you are making. Decreases are always visible and you will see that the stitches will slant either to the right or left. It is important to work them in pairs so that your work looks balanced, for instance when shaping a V-neck. Knitting together is the simplest means of decreasing.

Knitting two stitches together (K2tog or p2tog)

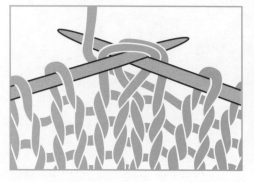

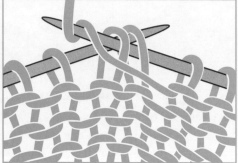

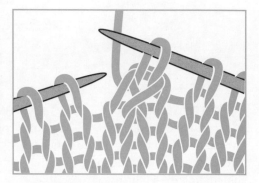

1 KNITWISE: Insert your right-hand needle through the front of the first two stitches on the left-hand needle. Knit together as one stitch.

2 PURLWISE: Insert your right-hand needle through the front of the first two stitches on the left-hand needle. Purl together as one stitch.

3 The decrease slants to the right if you knit the stitches together through the front of the loops, and to the left if you knit them together through the back.

Fishscale stitch

See rear cover photograph 4

This interesting textured stitch is suitable for intermediate knitters. A good body pattern for sweaters and cardigans, the K stitches at both ends of every row create a selvedge [selvage] for seaming (p. 168).

Multiple of 4 stitches plus 2
Row 1: (RS) K to end.
Row 2: K1, *yrn, p2, pass yrn over 2 p sts and off needle, p2; rep from * to last st, k1.
Row 3: as row 1.
Row 4: K1, *p2, yrn, p2, pass yrn over 2 p sts and off needle; rep from * to last st, k1.
Repeat rows 1 to 4 for the pattern.

Contrast is important to knitters with impaired vision. Use light-coloured needles when working with dark yarn and vice versa. It also helps to place a light-coloured cloth on your lap while knitting.

The slip stitch method is a little looser than knitting stitches together and produces a more decorative effect.

Slip stitch decrease in a knit row (sl 1, k1, psso)

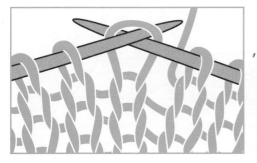

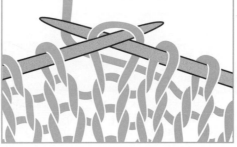

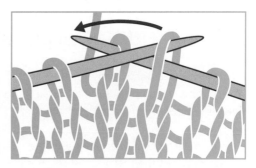

1 Insert your right-hand needle *knitwise* into the first stitch on the left-hand needle and transfer it from left to right without working the yarn.

2 Knit the next stitch on your left-hand needle in the usual way.

3 Slide the tip of your left-hand needle into the slipped stitch on your right and lift it over the stitch you have just knitted.

Slip stitch decrease in a purl row (sl 1, p1, psso)

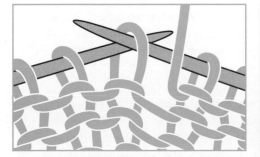

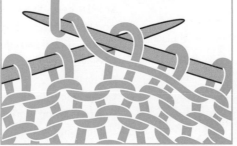

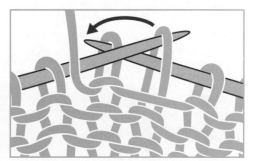

1 Insert your right-hand needle *purlwise* into the first stitch on the left-hand needle and transfer it from left to right without working the yarn.

2 Purl the next stitch on your left-hand needle in the usual way.

3 Slide the tip of your left-hand needle into the slipped stitch on your right and lift it over the stitch you have just purled.

KNITTING IN THE ROUND

Knitting in the round consists of working the yarn in a continuous spiral, therefore you have no seams to sew up. Another advantage is that the right side of the pattern always faces outwards, making it very clear to follow. The round method does mean certain reversals from 'normal' but the knitter soon adapts. For instance, to produce stocking stitch [stockinette], you will knit (k) every row; and garter stitch is produced by knitting and purling alternately.

Knitting with a circular needle

A circular needle holds many more stitches than an ordinary straight one, which makes it ideal for knitting large items like sweaters and skirts.

Work as if each pointed end is a separate needle. Slip a coloured marker between the first and last stitches of your cast-on and *most importantly* correct any twisted stitches by turning the entire cast-on edge towards the centre. When knitting the first stitch of the round, pull the yarn firmly to avoid a gap. Keep count by slipping your marker over on each round.

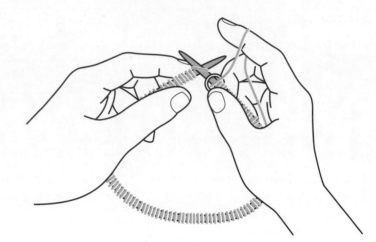

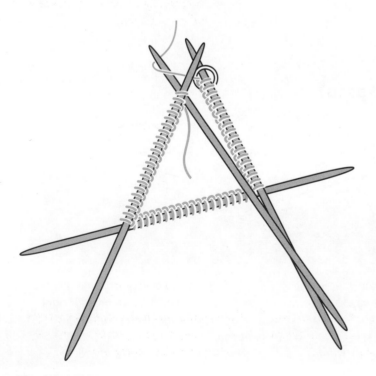

Knitting with three or more needles

Smaller items like socks and mittens are knitted on sets of double-pointed needles. These are particularly good for complex work like traditional Fair Isle patterns, collars and the individual fingers of gloves.

Cast on and divide the stitches evenly around the needles, keeping one free as the working needle. Slip a coloured marker between the first and last stitches of your cast-on. Knit one round making sure the first knitted stitch is close to the last needle and that no gaps will form. Continue like this, using the empty needles in turn to knit off. Hold the two working needles, meanwhile letting the other(s) hang at the back.

BUTTON EYELETS

Your choice of buttonhole depends on the item you are making. A simple eyelet is usually the first attempt, most often used on baby knits or as a slot for threading ribbon through. It also suits adult garments with small buttons. Work your eyelets at least two stitches in from the edge. (See also p. 182 for sewing a button loop on to a garment or bag.)

(See also p. 182 for sewing a button loop on to a garment or bag.)

Buy the buttons before you start so you know what size to make the holes. Avoid choosing any with rough or sharp edges; they can snag and wear through the yarn very quickly.

Simple or Chain eyelet (the 'yarn-over' buttonhole)

This will create a larger buttonhole if you use a thicker yarn.

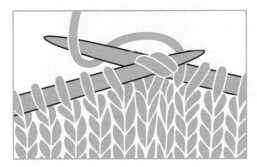

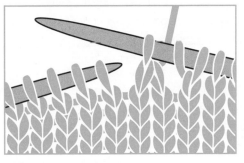

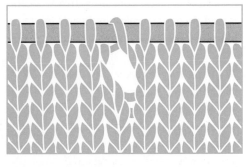

1 Work to the point where you want the buttonhole, bring the yarn to the front (yfwd /yo) then back over the needle in order to knit two stitches together (k2tog).

2 The overall number of stitches remains the same.

3 Knit the next row as normal in pattern, treating the yarn-over as an ordinary stitch. The eyelet is complete.

Open eyelet (the 'slip stitch' buttonhole)

A better option for threading ribbon.

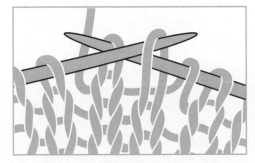

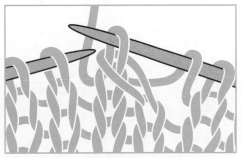

1 Work to the point where you want the buttonhole, then yarn over and slip (sl) the next stitch *knitwise* (sl 1 k-wise) onto your right-hand needle, knit one (k1).

2 With the tip of your left-hand needle, lift and pass the slip stitch over (psso) the one you have just knitted.

3 Knit the next row as normal in pattern, treating the yarn-over as an ordinary stitch. The eyelet is complete.

FINISHING

Blocking and pressing

Before assembling any knitted or crocheted garment, pattern pieces should be separately blocked and steamed. However, some fibres can be ruined by the touch of an iron, so consult the ball band from your yarn to see what is recommended. Some people only hold the iron above the damp cloth, close enough to create steam without setting it down at all.

Make an ironing pad from folded towels laid on a table and covered with a smooth cotton sheet. It should be big enough to take the largest piece laid out flat.

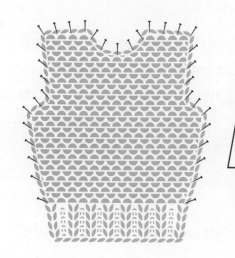

1 Place the piece wrong side up on the pad and *without over-stretching*, stab-pin it to the pad using plenty of long, non-rusting pins.

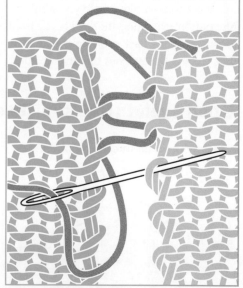

2 Set the iron according to the ball band, place a clean, damp cotton cloth over the piece then press briefly and gently. Move the iron by lifting, do not drag it over the surface.

Remove the pressing cloth and pins when the steam has cleared. Ease the piece into shape if necessary then allow it to dry completely.

Seams

Using the same yarn as the fabric, sew pieces together with a blunt-tipped yarn needle. There are two main types of seam:

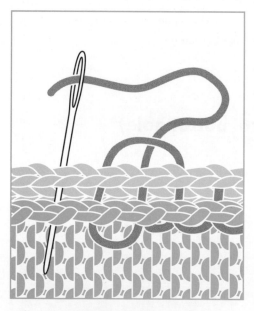

SEAMING ORDER

Always pin or tack [baste] first

1 Shoulder seams
2 Set sleeve heads in armholes
3 Side and sleeve seams in one go
4 Collar
5 Buttonbands
6 Pockets
7 Hems and casings

Follow pattern instructions if given

1 BACKSTITCH: Pin right sides together, with rows absolutely level and matching. Sew from right to left, about 6 mm [¼ in] from the edge. Make one stitch forward and then reverse, bringing the needle out again one stitch ahead of the first. A firm seam that forms a ridge on the wrong side of the garment.

2 LADDER STITCH: Edge-to-edge placing, right sides up, with rows absolutely level and matching. Sew alternately into the head of each edge stitch. Almost invisible if done well, this seam is ideal for lightweight fabrics.

DECORATING: WITH CROSS STITCH

Cross stitch work on knitting should be done to the same tension as the knitted fabric so that the garment is not pulled out of shape. To avoid splitting the knitted yarn, use a blunt-ended tapestry or darning needle with an eye large enough to take the yarn. As well as single motifs, you can use cross stitch to add letters – we have supplied an alphabet chart below as a guide. Each square on the chart represents a single cross stitch.

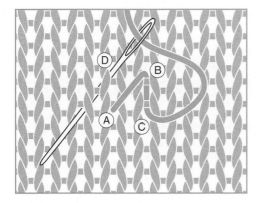

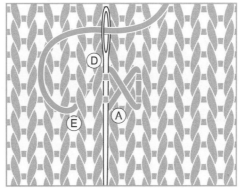

To work longer rows of cross stitch more quickly, you can work end to end in single diagonals and complete the stitches by crossing them on return.

1 Secure the end of the yarn at the back of the work with a knot or backstitch before bringing your needle through at point A. Stitch a diagonal from A to B. Bring your needle out at point C and insert again at D.

2 To complete the cross stitch, bring your needle out at E. To continue, insert the needle again at D and bring out again at A.

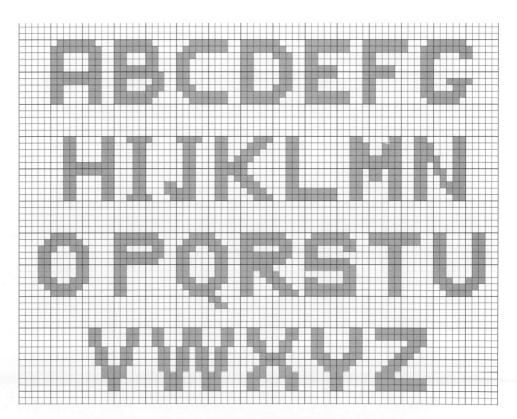

DECORATING: WITH SWISS DARNING

This form of embroidery imitates the knitting underneath and should be worked to the same tension. It is quick to do and produces a raised design because it forms a double fabric. As well as single motifs, you can use Swiss darning to add contrasting stripes or letters and even to reinforce areas of a garment, like elbows or knees. To avoid splitting the knitted yarn, use a blunt-ended tapestry or darning needle with an eye large enough to take the yarn.

To work horizontally

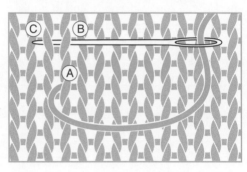

1 Secure the end of the yarn at the back of the work with a knot or backstitch before bringing your needle through at point A. Insert the needle at B, under the base of the stitch above, and bring out at C.

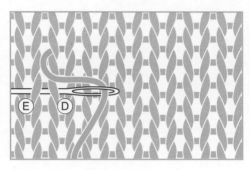

2 Insert your needle at D and bring it out at E, ready for the next stitch.

To work vertically

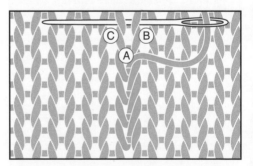

1 Secure the end of the yarn at the back of the work with a knot or backstitch before bringing your needle through at point A. Insert the needle at B, under the base of the stitch above, and bring out at C.

2 Take the needle under the head of the stitch below and bring it out at D, ready for the next stitch upward.

ATTACHING BEADS AND SEQUINS

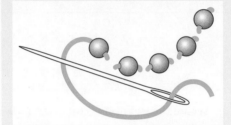

Secure the yarn at the back of the work. Bring the yarn through to the right side and thread on one bead. Push your needle back through, or close to, the same place. Advance one stitch on the wrong side and bring the yarn through ready for the next bead.

Use matching sewing thread and secure at the back. Hold the sequin flat against the right side and push the needle up through the centre. Back stitch over the right hand edge, come up on the left hand edge and back stitch down through the centre. Repeat with the next sequin. Sequins should not be used on items for children under 3.

DECORATING: WITH TASSELS AND FRINGES

It's easy to make tassels and fringes from matching or contrasting yarn for both knitted and crocheted items. You will need a rectangle of card that measures about 1 cm [½ in] more than the desired length of the tassel or fringe.

Tassels

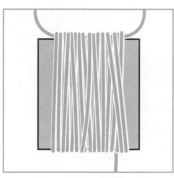 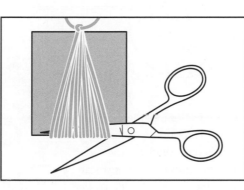 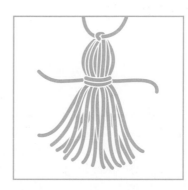

1 Wrap the yarn around the card. Thread one strand, 30 cm [12 in] long, under the top loops.

2 Tie this strand tightly at the top; the ends can be knotted or crocheted later, or threaded up for sewing. Cut all the tassel loops free at the lower edge.

3 Take another length of yarn and wind firmly round the loose strands to form the tassel head. Finish with a secure knot. Thread the ends into a yarn needle and work neatly into the centre of the tassel before trimming level.

Knotted fringe

Wrap the yarn around the card, as for tassels, then cut along one edge to produce the strands of the fringe. Group these into as many bundles as you need.

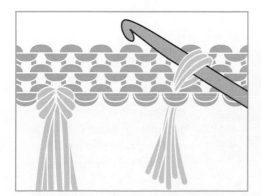  

1 Insert a crochet hook through the fabric edge from back to front. Loop a bundle of yarn in half, hook and pull through to the back so the loop is on one side and the cut ends on the other.

2 With hook or fingers, draw the cut ends through the loop.

3 Pull gently but firmly to form a neat knot on the fabric edge. Repeat at regular intervals. Trim ends level as necessary.

DECORATING: WITH POMPOMS

Pompoms make a cheerful addition to winter clothes, especially on hats and scarves. You could buy a plastic pompom maker but this method recycles both card and small amounts of yarn at no cost at all.

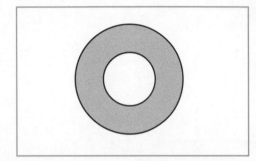

1 Cut two matching circles from thin card (cereal boxes or old postcards) to the desired size of the pompom. Cut a hole in the exact centre of each, measuring about one third of the diameter of the outer circle. Take care to prepare these rings accurately or your pompom will not be a perfect sphere.

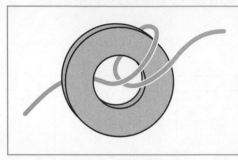

2 Put the card circles together and start winding yarn around them through the hole in the centre. Work to cover the rings evenly; if the yarn runs out just start winding on another length. Multicoloured pompoms are an excellent way of using up lots of short scraps of yarn.

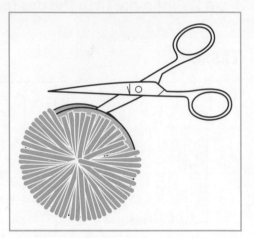

3 Once the centre hole is filled (use a blunt-tipped yarn needle when it gets very tight) take your scissors and cut through the outer strands until you can push the blade in between the two layers of card. Cut through all the yarn right around the edge.

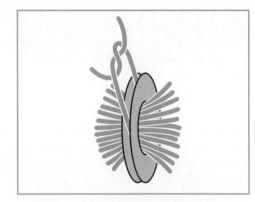

4 Take a length of yarn 30–45 cm [12–18 in] long and slide it between the cardboard rings. Knot it as tightly as you can around the centre of the pompom, wrap round once or twice, pull and tie again but do not cut it. Then remove the card from either side.

5 Fluff up the pompom and trim smooth if necessary. The long ends of yarn can be knotted or crocheted into a decorative hanger; or you can cut one strand and thread up the other for sewing directly on to a garment.

PART THREE:
CROCHET METHODS AND TECHNIQUES

HOLDING YARN AND HOOK

There are two ways to hold a crochet hook. Both are equally good, so choose whichever suits you best.

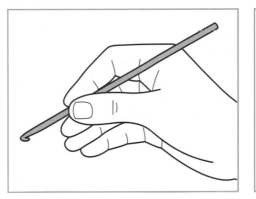

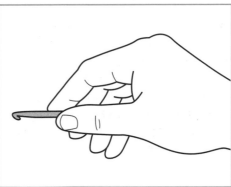

The pencil position

Hold the flat part of the hook between your thumb and index finger as if writing with a pencil.

The knife position

Curl your hand round the hook with your thumb on the flat part and the index finger pressing on the top as if holding a knife.

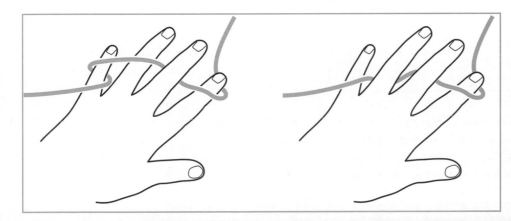

In crochet, the working yarn is fed through the opposite hand from the one holding the hook. Threading it through the fingers helps to control the tension and allows the yarn to pass smoothly from hand to hook. There are no hard and fast rules – use the method most comfortable for you. Turn to p. 151 for how to make a tension [gauge] sample.

CHAIN FOUNDATIONS

All crochet begins with a single loop on the hook. This is the initial working loop and, unlike knitting, is not counted as a stitch. From this loop comes the foundation chain on which the next *row* (for straight work) or *round* (for circular or spiral work) is built.

Chain foundation row

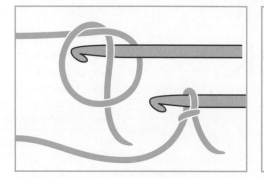 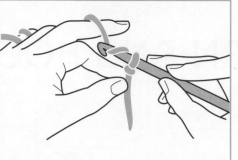 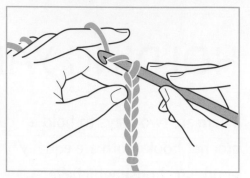

1 Make a slip loop in the end of the yarn and tighten round the shank of the hook. Leave a tail of 15 cm [6 in].

2 Holding the hook in your right hand, grip the knot of the slip loop between your left thumb and index finger (or middle, if preferred). Twist the hook under and over the working yarn; this is called 'yarn round hook' (yrh).

3 Draw the hook with the yarn back through the slip loop to form your first chain stitch (ch). Repeat as required, moving your left hand up to hold the work firmly as you go.

Chain foundation ring

As a basis for crochet in the round, the closed ring method is the one most often used, but see also p. 184.

Make a short foundation chain as above; for example, the pattern states 'ch 7.' Then insert the hook into the first chain stitch you did. Work yarn round hook (yrh) and draw the new loop back through to close the ring with a slip stitch (ss /sl st).

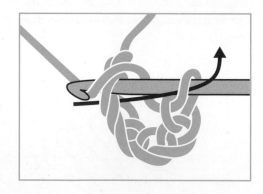

Working in the round means you do not turn your work between rounds; the right side is always facing you. Depending on your pattern, you might work in a spiral, where you will need coloured markers to mark your progress. Or you might crochet a series of rounds joined with a slip stitch, as above; in which case, before starting the next round you will have to make a very short vertical chain (t-ch) to match the height of the following stitches (p. 179).

BASIC STITCHES

Before going further, we should learn the differences between UK and US crochet stitch names, especially as we increasingly share our patterns – new and vintage – through the internet. In this book we are using UK terms with the US equivalents in square brackets [ ] alongside. The abbreviations for UK and US stitches appear in parentheses ( ) separated by a slash / if shared.

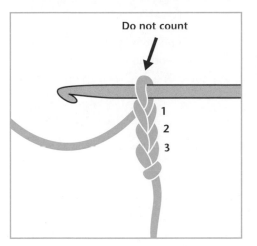

Do not count

1
2
3

Chain stitch (ch)

This is used so often that it is essential to know how to count chains properly. The working loop that remains on your hook is never counted as a stitch. There are just three chains in this diagram, and if a pattern instructs you to crochet into the second chain from the hook, you can see how to count your way to it.

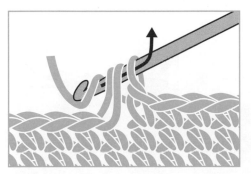

Single crochet (sc) [Slip stitch (sl st)]

From here on you will see that the clue to all the different crochet stitches is the number of times the yarn is wrapped round the hook.

Insert the hook into the next stitch. Yarn round hook (yrh /yo) and draw the new loop back through. One loop remains on the hook. This simple stitch adds little height to the work and is most commonly used to join rounds (see opposite).

Double crochet (dc) [Single crochet (sc)]

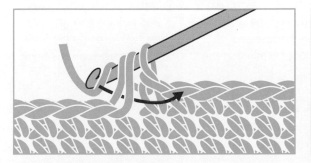

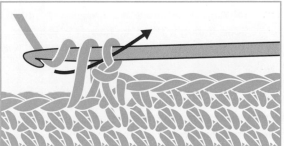

1 Insert the hook into the next stitch. Yarn round hook (yrh /yo) and draw the new loop through. There are now two loops on your hook.

2 Yarn round hook (yrh /yo) again and pull the working yarn through both loops. One loop remains on the hook.

Half treble crochet (htr) [Half double crochet (hdc)]

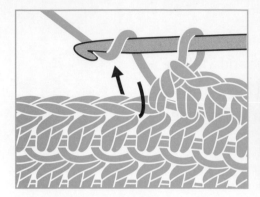 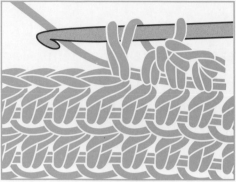 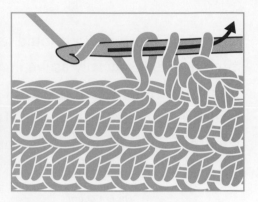

1 Yarn round hook (yrh /yo) and insert the hook into the next stitch.

2 Yarn round hook (yrh /yo) and draw the new loop through. There are now three loops on your hook.

3 Yarn round hook (yrh /yo) again and pull the working yarn through the three loops. One loop remains on the hook.

This stitch is a little shorter than treble crochet and taller than double crochet.

Treble crochet (tr) [Double crochet (dc)]

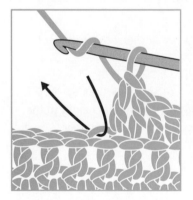 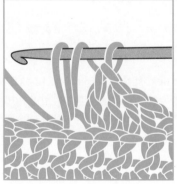 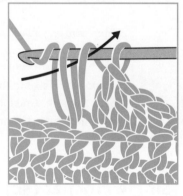 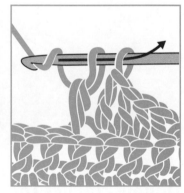

1 Yarn round hook (yrh /yo) and insert the hook into the next stitch.

2 Yarn round hook (yrh /yo) again and draw the new loop through. There are now three loops on your hook.

3 Yarn round hook (yrh /yo) again and pull the working yarn through the first two loops. Two loops remain on the hook.

4 Yarn round hook (yrh /yo) and pull the yarn through the last two loops on the hook. One loop remains on the hook.

Treble crochet is twice the height of double crochet. This is one of the stitches most frequently used in making granny squares (p. 184–6).

Double treble crochet (dtr) [Triple crochet (tr)]

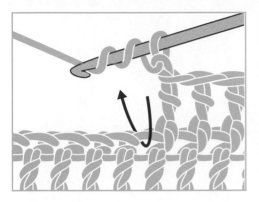

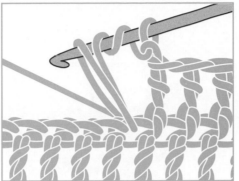

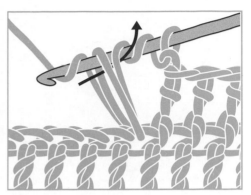

1 Yarn round hook twice (yrh /yo) and insert the hook into the next stitch.

2 Yarn round hook (yrh /yo) again and pull the yarn through the stitch. There are now four loops on your hook.

3 Yarn round hook (yrh /yo) and pull the yarn through the first two loops. Three loops remain on the hook.

Double treble crochet is taller than treble crochet. It is another stitch often used for granny squares (p. 184–6).

4 Yarn round hook (yrh /yo) and pull the yarn through the next two loops. Two loops remain on the hook.

5 Yarn round hook (yrh /yo) and pull the yarn through the last two loops. One loop remains on the hook.

Triple treble crochet (ttr) [Double triple crochet (dtr)]

Work as for UK double treble crochet but yarn round hook (yrh /yo) three times so there are five loops altogether on the hook. Then work loops off in pairs as for double treble [triple] crochet.

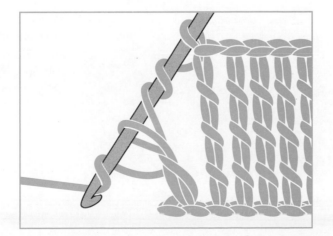

BASIC STITCH VARIATIONS

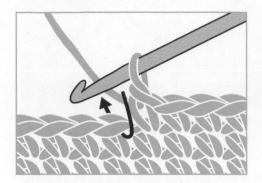

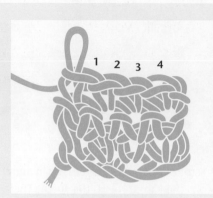

As a general rule, once you have worked over the foundation chain and are into the stitch pattern, you should always insert the crochet hook under *both* top loops of the stitch in the previous row, unless otherwise instructed.

Those top loops also offer the easiest way to count your stitches.

By inserting the crochet hook in different ways, it is possible to produce a wide range of textural effects from the basic stitches. The simplest variation is to work into either the front or back top loop, as shown right and far right. Then try working the back and front loops alternately within the same row.

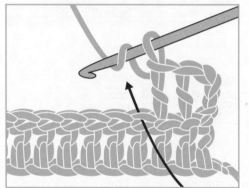

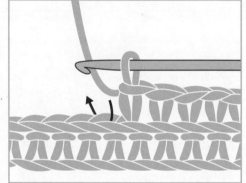

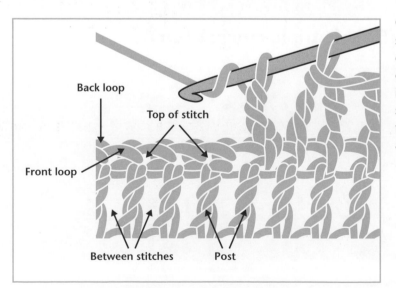

Back loop

Top of stitch

Front loop

Between stitches

Post

Other variations involve working between stitches and around the 'posts' or 'stems' of stitches – the possibilities are virtually endless. The comprehensive diagram left identifies different parts of the crochet stitch. For clarity we have used the double treble [triple] crochet although the points apply to all crochet stitches.

TURNING CHAINS

At the start of individual rows and rounds, a certain number of 'turning chains' (t-ch) are required to raise the hook to the height of the stitch being worked. The instructions might read: 'Ch 2. Turn' at the end of the previous row; *or* 'Turn' at the end of the previous row and 'Ch. 2' at the start of the next. They both mean the same and either way the chains will form the edge of the crocheted fabric.

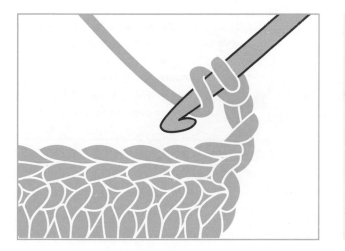

TABLE OF TURNING CHAINS (T-CH)

UK STITCH [US]	NO. OF CHAINS
Double crochet [Single]	ch 1 or 2 to turn
Half treble [Half double]	ch 2 to turn
Treble [Double]	ch 3 to turn
Double treble [Triple]	ch 4 to turn
Triple treble [Double triple]	ch 5 to turn

Turning chains count as the first stitch in each new row. To compensate, the first stitch in the actual pattern should be worked into the top of the *second* stitch of the previous row. If you do not miss [skip] the first stitch after a turning chain, you will in fact increase a stitch (p. 180). Printed patterns give full instructions.

ADDING NEW YARN WITHOUT KNOTTING

Here's how to join fresh yarn or add a new colour at the start of a row if you want horizontal stripes.

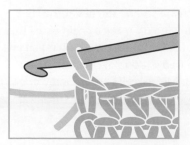

Work the new yarn with the old just before completing the final stitch of the previous row. Then drop the old so you work the turning chain in the new colour. Keep the old yarn to the wrong side with a long enough tail for weaving in.

INCREASING

When making a garment, you need to shape the fabric and this means adding stitches. The decorative nature of crochet also involves increasing and decreasing in the creation of patterns and textures. Printed patterns carry the necessary instructions.

The simplest increase in crochet is to work two (or more) stitches into the same stitch; this is less noticeable within a row than at the ends. If more than one increase is required per row, they are usually spaced evenly throughout. Our example uses treble [double] crochet stitch worked on a foundation chain.

Working twice into the same stitch (Inc 1)

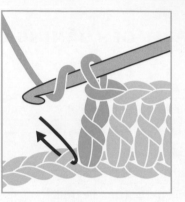 

If the pattern calls for a greater increase, keep adding stitches at the same point. It is best to count and make sure you have the correct number of stitches by the end of the row.

1 Work to the point where you want the increase and make your first stitch through the top loop(s) of the stitch below.

2 Work another stitch in the same loop(s). You have now increased the row by one stitch.

Three more methods of increasing

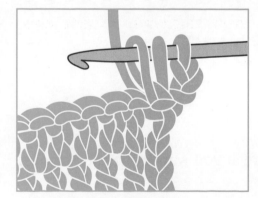  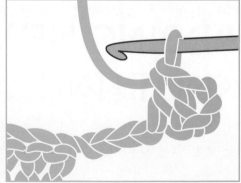

1 At the beginning of a row with a turning chain, instead of missing [skipping] the first stitch, work your increase in there.

2 At the end of a row, work in pattern up to the last two stitches. Work twice in the next stitch, then work the final stitch as usual into the top of the turning chain of the previous row.

3 To increase several stitches at the start of a row (eg 6), make a chain equal to one less stitch (eg 5), plus the turning chain (eg 3 for a treble [double] crochet), that is, a total of 8. Miss [skip] 3 chains and work 1 treble [double] into each of the remaining 5 new chains, giving an increase of 6 stitches, *including the turning chain.*

DECREASING

Like increasing, decreasing is also necessary to shape the fabric that you are making. The simplest method is to miss [skip] one or more stitches but this may leave noticeable holes. Unless you are aiming for an eyelet effect, it is best to decrease by crocheting stitches together.

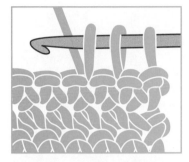 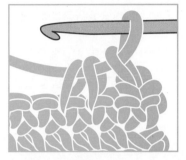 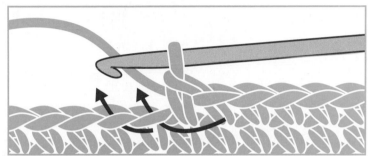

1 Work to the point where you want the decrease and insert the hook into the next stitch, yarn round hook (yrh /yo) and draw the loop through. Repeat in the next stitch. There are now three loops on the hook.

2 Yarn round hook (yrh /yo) and draw the loop through all three loops. One stitch has been decreased.

3 FOR AN 'INVISIBLE DECREASE': insert the hook into the front loops only of the next two stitches. Yarn round hook (yrh /yo) and draw the loop through both front loops. Yarn round hook (yrh /yo) and draw the loop through both loops on the hook.

GEOMETRIC SHAPES

Geometric shapes can be crocheted by increasing and decreasing the basic stitches in different ways.

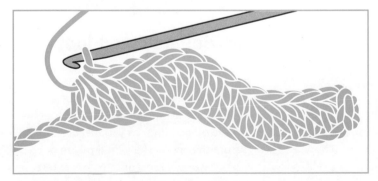 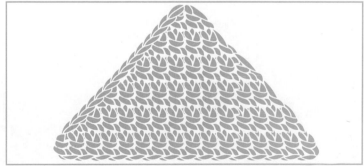

Chevrons (zigzags, ripples or waves) are created by increasing and decreasing the same stitch alternately at the same place in each row. The fabric pattern is ideal for scarves and blankets. *See rear cover photograph 5.*

Simple triangles are formed by working a foundation chain and making a single decrease at the end of every row, plus a decrease at the beginning of every third row

FASTENINGS

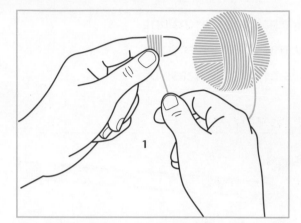

Making yarn buttons

Buttons can be knitted or crocheted but this method is even simpler. Wrap the yarn round your finger six times. Slip the loops off and wrap yarn around the middle before folding in half and wrapping more to form a firm ball. Cut the yarn to a 40 cm [16 in] tail. Thread up a yarn needle and sew through the ball a few times to secure it. Use the rest to sew the button on.

Making a crochet buttonhole

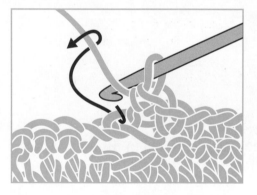

Form the buttonhole three or four stitches in from the edge of your piece, ideally within two rows of double [single] crochet for stability. Make two chains or more for the hole, which should have to stretch slightly over the button. Miss [skip] the same number of stitches in the row below. Re-insert your hook and work on. Resume pattern on the next row.

Sewing a button loop

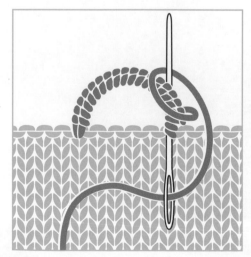
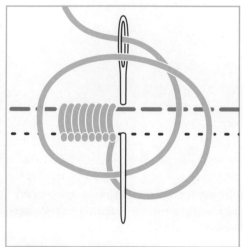

Loops make good alternative fastenings for clothes and bags. Sew them on the edge of one side, to align with a button or toggle on the other. Thread a yarn needle and secure the end of the yarn firmly to one point by oversewing once or twice; test for size with the button, then loop it over to a second fixing point. Carry on looping and securing the yarn two or three times, before buttonhole stitching neatly to hold the strands together.

EDGINGS

Edgings give your crochet a neat finish and combine well with knitting too. Either work them directly on to a piece or in a separate strip to be sewn on afterwards. For a firm edge, use a smaller size hook than for the main item.

Double [single] crochet edging

A basic border that neatens, strengthens and can cover float threads and loose ends. It makes a good foundation for more decorative edgings. It can also be worked with chain button loops at intervals.

Picot edging

A simple applied edging, sufficiently small-scale for baby clothes.

This example of triple picot is worked over a foundation row of single [double] crochet as follows: *5 sc [dc], (ch3, ss [sl st] in 3rd ch from hook) 3 times, then ss [sl st] into top of last sc [dc] made; repeat from * to end.

PROJECT: CROCHET SHAWL

Diagonal shell pattern

See rear cover photograph 6

Multiples of 5 stitches plus 2

For a large baby shawl approx 90 cm [36 in] wide, using size 6.0 mm [J] hook and 3 ply baby double knitting yarn, chain 142.

For a smaller shawl approx 70 cm [28 in] wide, using the same hook and yarn, chain 112.

Row 1: (RS) 3 tr [dc] in 3rd chain from hook, *skip 3 ch, 1 dc [sc], ch 3, 3tr in next ch; rep from * to last 4 ch, skip 3 ch, 1 dc [sc] in final ch, turn.
Row 2: Ch 3, 3 tr in 3rd chain from hook, *skip 3 tr [dc], (1 dc [sc], ch 3, 3 tr [dc]) in 3 ch space; rep from * to last 3 tr, skip 2 tr, 1 dc [sc] in final tr, turn.
Row 2 forms the pattern. Repeat Row 2 until work reaches the desired length.

This pattern produces a decorative edge of its own.

Shawl dimensions are approximate. Results depend on your stitch tension as well as any variation in hook size or yarn thickness. Work a sample square first (p. 151), based on chain 27.

Shell edging

See rear cover photograph 7

Another popular style, which makes for a deeper trim. This is a simple version: 1ss [sl st] into 1st st, *miss [skip] 2 sts, 5tr [dc] into next st, miss [skip] 2 sts, 1ss [sl st] into next st, repeat from * to end.

Crochet with fine threads on steel hooks is a type of lacemaking, and a surprisingly quick way of creating trimmings for clothes and household linens like pillow cases and table napkins.

GRANNY SQUARES

They look complicated, worked in so many colours, but traditional granny squares are not difficult and provide an excellent introduction to crocheting in rounds. Economical to produce – using all your odds and ends of yarn – they make up easily into rugs, shawls, cushions, even clothes.

The main stitches are treble [double] crochet, chains, and slip stitch for joining the rounds, yet many different arrangements are possible. Create some for yourself after a little practice. Going further, the basic structure extends to triangles, hexagons and flower shapes. The square always begins with a foundation ring, usually the chain foundation (p. 174). But there is another type, for use when your pattern calls for a neat, closed centre.

Yarn loop foundation

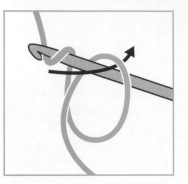  

1 Make a slip loop as shown, leaving a tail about 10 cm [4 in] long.

2 Work the first round in pattern, usually double [single] crochet stitches all round the circle *over both the loop and the tail.*

3 Pull the tail end firmly to draw the circle together.

Starting a round on a chain foundation ring

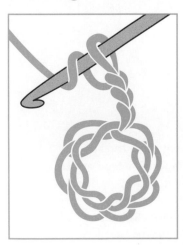 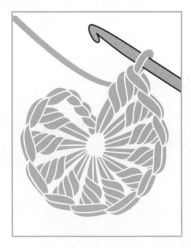

1 After joining your ring with a slip stitch (ss /sl st), make a turning chain (t-ch) long enough to accommodate your first pattern stitch.

2 Our example shows 11tr [dc] worked into the ring so that the chain stitches are completely enclosed. To close the round, work a slip stitch (ss /sl st) into the top of the turning chain (t-ch). You must make the required turning chain every time before starting the next round.

A granny square worked in stages

Here is the plan for a simple granny square crocheted in a single colour.

1 The initial trebles [doubles] around the foundation ring are spaced and linked by chains. A group of three trebles [doubles] is often called a 'cluster'.

2 In the second round, after the required turning chain, trebles are worked over those chain links.

3 The pattern is repeated and so the chequered effect builds. This pattern is in a style called 'filet', meaning 'net'.

Joining granny squares will go better if you have given each one a good firm edging (p. 183). You may either sew them together edge-to-edge (p. 168) or make a flat slip-stitch seam using your crochet hook. This is done wrong side up, working 1ss [sl st] into alternate edges.

FINISHING YOUR WORK

If you have used different-coloured yarns, weave in all the ends neatly.

When an individual piece is complete, cut the yarn, leaving a tail of 15 cm [6 in]. Slide the final loop off the hook, slip the yarn end through and pull gently until it closes. Thread the tail into a blunt-tipped yarn needle and weave it into the edge for about 7 cm [3 in].

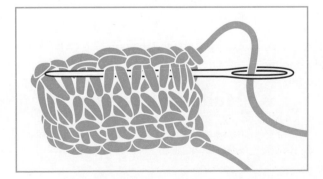

PROJECT: GRANNY SQUARE CUSHION

With the granny square design on page 185, you can create a cushion cover with a handmade charm of its own. In vibrant primaries or restful tints, all one colour or sharp black and white, the choice is yours.

For the traditional look, take colours from across the spectrum and work each round in a different colour. If you use black on the final round, it will have a stained glass window effect.

These squares can be subtle too. Choose one light and one dark shade of the main colour in your room. Work a pale neutral edging around each square, for the look that complements a contemporary interior.

For this project, take a 45x45 cm [18x18 in] square cushion pad and make 16 granny squares to cover one side of it. Each square will measure 10 cm [4 in] and consist of 4 rounds worked with a 4.50 mm [US 7] hook and double knitting yarn or equivalent.

If you change colours with each round, be prepared to have a good number of tails to weave in (p. 185). If you neaten each square as you go, you won't have a huge task at the end. You must also decide whether or not to give each square a double [single] crochet edging when the four rounds are finished (p. 183). It does give the square a strong margin and helps when it comes to stitching them all together.

The squares will be attached not to the cushion pad itself but to a cloth cover, which is readily made from an average-sized pillow case, cut shorter to fit and finished along the open edge with a zip fastener, hook-and-loop tape, or buttoned flap-over.

Single-colour square

Make foundation chain of 6 and close with ss [sl st] (see p. 174)

Round 1 (see p. 184):   Ch 3 counts as first tr [dc], 2 tr [dc] into ring, ch 2, (3 tr [dc] into ring, ch 2) three times. Join with ss [sl st] to the third of the first 3ch.

Round 2:   Ch 2, (3tr [dc], ch 2, 3tr [dc]) into first 2ch-sp to form corner, * ch 1, (3tr [dc], ch 2, 3tr [dc]) into next 2ch-sp; rep from * twice more. Join with ss [sl st] to the first of the first 2ch.

Round 3:   Ch 3 counts as first tr [dc], 2 tr [dc] into first ch-sp to left of ss [sl st] of previous round, ch 1, *(3tr [dc], ch 2, 3tr [dc]) into 2ch-sp, ch 1, 3 tr [dc] into 1ch-sp, ch1; rep from * twice more, (3tr [dc], ch 2, 3tr [dc]) into last 2ch-sp, ch1. Join with ss [sl st] to the third of the first 3ch.

Round 4:   Ch2, 3 tr [dc] into next 1ch-sp, ch 1, *(3tr [dc], ch 2, 3tr [dc]) into 2ch-sp, ch 1, (3 tr [dc] into next 1ch-sp, ch1) twice; rep from * twice more, (3tr [dc], ch 2, 3tr [dc]) into last 2ch-sp, ch1, 3tr [dc]) into last 1ch-sp. Join with ss [sl st] to the first of the first 2ch.

Cut yarn, pull end through loop on hook and pull firmly to fasten off.

Multi-coloured square

Make foundation chain and work Round 1 as for single-colour square. Cut yarn and fasten off.

Round 2:   Join new colour yarn to any 2ch-sp with ss [sl st], ch 3 to count as first tr [dc], 2 tr [dc] into same ch-sp, * ch1, (3tr [dc], ch 2, 3tr [dc]) into next 2ch-sp to form corner; rep from * twice more, ch 1, 3 tr [dc] into same 2 ch-sp as beg of round, ch 2. Join with ss [sl st] to the third of the first 3ch. Cut yarn and fasten off.

Round 3:   Join new colour yarn to any 2ch-sp with ss [sl st], ch 3 to count as first tr [dc], 2 tr [dc] into same 2 ch-sp, * ch1, 3 tr [dc] into next 1 ch-sp, ch 1, (3tr [dc], ch 2, 3tr [dc]) into next 2ch-sp; rep from * twice more, ch 1, 3 tr [dc] into next 1 ch-sp, ch 1, 3 tr [dc] into same 2 ch-sp as beg of round, ch 2. Join with ss [sl st] to the third of the first 3ch. Cut yarn and fasten off.

Round 4:   Join new colour yarn to any 2ch-sp with ss [sl st], ch 3 to count as first tr [dc], 2 tr [dc] into same 2 ch-sp, * (ch1, 3 tr [dc] into next 1 ch-sp) twice, ch 1, (3tr [dc], ch 2, 3tr [dc]) into next 2ch-sp; rep from * twice more, (ch 1, 3 tr [dc] into next 1 ch-sp) twice, ch 1, 3 tr [dc] into same 2 ch-sp as beg of round, ch 2. Join with ss [sl st] to the third of the first 3ch. Cut yarn and fasten off.

When all the tails are woven in, add a double [single] crochet edging (p. 183) to each square or join them straightaway with ladder stitch (p. 168). Alternatively, slip-stitch them together with a crochet hook (p. 185).

Finally, hem-stitch your piece around the edge of the base cover with sewing thread.

Add more rounds for larger squares by increasing 3tr [dc] and 1 ch along each side. Results depend on stitch tension and any variation in hook size or yarn.

AFTERCARE

Snags

If you have caught and pulled a loop on something like a nail, don't be tempted to cut it off – your knitting or crochet will unravel. If the snag is minor, work it back into the fabric with a little gentle flexing and stretching of the surrounding stitches. If you have snagged a long loop, push it through to the wrong side using a yarn needle or crochet hook.

Stains

Deal quickly with stains. Do not rub the affected area because friction damages yarn fibres and can leave an obvious patch. Oil-based marks should be tackled from the wrong side of the fabric with a proper solvent; follow the manufacturer's instructions. Most stains – apart from oil and grease – are treatable with a clean sponge or tea towel soaked in cold water, hot water will 'set' a stain. For tea, coffee and alcohol, some people recommend carbonated water; this should be plain without added sugar or flavours. A stubborn mark may respond to neat liquid soap, the type sold for washing wool and silk but try this remedy only if you are certain the yarn is colour-fast. Mud should always be allowed to dry first so that the excess can be brushed off.

Laundering

First, study the care symbols on the ball band (p. 149) and find the recommended temperature. It's useful to keep one band of everything that you make, with the colour and type of item written on the back. Don't put wool to soak unless you intend to shrink or felt it (see Recycling). Wool fibres have tiny scales that bond together permanently with water and heat (beware, a too-hot tumble drier will have the same effect).

Whether hand- or machine washing, avoid using washing powder either on crochet lace or items with a high wool content. The cleansing agents in liquid soaps are designed to work at low temperatures and won't leave a powdery deposit. Liquid soap works equally well on man-made fibres, especially in hard water areas.

Turn all garments inside out and – if machine washing – place inside a mesh bag to prevent any stretching or tangling (a pillow case secured at the top with an elastic band will do). Modern machines have a range of wash and spin programs for woollens and synthetics, use them with confidence so long as it says 'machine washable' on the ball band. The wool program applies to yarns labelled 'pure new wool', 'washable' and 'pre-shrunk'; other types such as angora should go on the handwash program, which ensures the gentlest treatment with the least agitation.

Fabric softener is not greatly recommended for natural yarn fibres. Too much of it relaxes stitch tension and results in loss of shape. In the case of chenille, it encourages shedding of the short fibres and should not be used at all. However, conditioner does help to reduce static electricity with synthetics.

If washing by hand, place the item in a bowl and work up a lather with gentle pressing and squeezing, don't rub or twist. Rinse in several changes of water. WOOLLENS SHOULD BE RINSED IN WARM WATER, ACRYLICS ALWAYS IN COLD.

When you take the item from the drum or bowl, support it as you transfer it to a dry towel and then roll them both up together to remove the excess moisture. Do not wring. Turn garments right side out.

Using a work surface or a flat-topped airing rack, spread another (dry) towel and lay the item out flat so the moisture evaporates evenly from the entire surface. Gently pull it into shape; don't let garment sleeves dangle, fasten all buttons and fold collars down.

If you have a dehumidifier, this will speed the drying process, otherwise keep your knitting and crochet away from direct heat or harsh sunlight. Never peg items out to dry or hang them on hangers; clothes pegs leave deep marks and all the moisture runs downward so things stretch and dry unevenly. If your item is not completely dry after 24 hours, turn it over and lay it out once more.

Iron only if indicated and always use steam in combination with a pressing cloth on the reverse side of the fabric. Crochet lace will require pressing, treat it the same as embroidery, again using a pressing cloth. Alternatively stretch and pin it out to dry flat with the same long, rustproof pins as for blocking (p. 168).

STORAGE

These notes apply as much to bagfuls of unused yarn as to any finished clothes, blankets, toys or accessories. Check your stash regularly and invest in clear ziplock bags for storage.

The chief enemies of knitted fabrics are damp and insects – the clothes moth is principally attracted to woollen fibres. The golden rule is always to put everything away clean. Dust, dirt and perspiration can harm and discolour fibres of all kinds – synthetics as well as natural – and both moths and moulds feed readily on dirt.

Don't pack items too closely in a confined area, allow air to circulate around them. Precious heirlooms like christening gowns and shawls should be laundered or dry cleaned, then interleaved with plenty of acid-free tissue paper and stored immediately in zipped cotton cases. Keep your knitwear and blankets folded neatly and well-protected in drawers, chests and cupboards (even in suitcases), or inside zipped covers and lidded plastic boxes for long-term storage. You can tape around the box lids for extra protection. Label the containers, you almost certainly won't remember exactly what you have placed inside.

When checking stored items, it is a good idea to shake them out occasionally and refold so that creases don't become permanent.

The clothes moth is only about 7 mm [1/4 in] long and pale brown in colour. It tends to hover around the area of infestation and its feeble fluttery flight makes it fairly easy to swat. Stay vigilant, clothes moths will always seek out the darkest corners, creeping through cracks into drawers and cupboards (they love the nooks and crannies of wooden furniture), and it is a wise precaution to look every couple of weeks if you aren't opening them regularly; keep disturbing the moth's potential habitat and they won't settle.

The female lays an average of fifty eggs during a period of two or three weeks, then she dies. Males, however, outlive the females and continue mating for the rest of their lives. Eggs hatch in a week to ten days, and it is the larvae that do all the damage, chewing through not only woollen fabric but also silk, fur, feathers and stored yarn. Moths will even feed on synthetics or fabrics such as cotton, if they are blended with wool. Examine the concealed areas of garments: the seams, under collars, cuffs and fastenings. In summer, take woollens out into the sunshine, larvae hate exposure to light and will drop off an article in order to find another hiding place.

Nowadays, the war against the moth no longer involves pungent camphor; there are pleasantly scented alternatives like oil of citronella, cedarwood blocks and lavender sachets, although these should be renewed from time to time. Modern mothballs change colour when they need replacing.

Spray insecticides should be used with care, and not near silks or rayon, because they are generally oil-based and could mark delicate fabrics.

Good housekeeping is fundamental and the vacuum cleaner nozzle is your most effective weapon against larvae lurking under heavy furniture or in warm, dark heating vents. Empty the dust bag or cylinder often and dispose of the contents completely, they may contain eggs that will continue to hatch and cause fresh infestation in the house. Although most people manage to solve their moth problems themselves, some infestations persist and call for help from professional pest controllers.

Guard against mould and mildew by making sure laundered items are completely dry before they are stored away. And keep them in dry, well-aired spaces, preferably not in lofts or cellars. Low-powered cupboard heaters and dehumidifiers will help to reduce condensation problems.

RECYCLING

Unravelling yarn

Re-using the yarn from old knitwear is an economy measure from World War II that fits well with the current culture of recycling. Unfashionable hand-knits found in charity shops – or any of your own that have lost their appeal – can be given a new lease of life and provide enough yarn for smaller items like hats, scarves and gloves. The yarn in machine-made knitwear is harder to unpick because the pieces have been assembled with an overlocker [serger], however, there should still be one or two 'normal' seams where you can open up and find an end to unravel.

A word about buying secondhand knitwear: take the trouble to inspect it and make sure you are not about to waste your time and money. If the wool feels even slightly felted it will not unravel; it has been damaged by heat and will never be the same again. Unfortunately, some fibres are too fragile to be worth your effort; chenille will shed its velvet everywhere as soon as you set about unravelling.

Start by unpicking the seams of the garment (collars are a good place to begin), taking care not to snip into the fabric itself. Now unravel the knitting downward from the cast-off end of each section. You may not be able to unravel each section entirely without cutting the yarn free at some point. Wind the yarn into a ball as you go to prevent yourself from – quite literally – getting into a tangle. The next step is to convert the yarn ball into a coiled skein by rewinding it around the back of a dining chair.

When you have finished and before removing it from the chair, tie your skein in three or four places with short lengths of yarn, this holds the coils together for washing. Hand wash in warm soapy water, swishing the skein about gently to loosen any dirt. Rinse thoroughly, shake it, and either hang it up or lay it flat to dry naturally.

When it is completely dry, rewind the skein into balls – not too tightly. Don't worry about the yarn breaks, they can be joined as you knit something entirely new from your recycled yarn.

Felting

Felting creates an entirely different fabric out of old woollen garments, plain or patterned. The stitch definition disappears, leaving a smoother, flattened surface. Do check the label on the garment first, if it says 'pre-shrunk- or 'machine washable' the technique won't work. On the other hand, the instruction to 'dry clean only' promises success. The condition of the item does not matter since you can cut badly worn or stained patches away from the finished felt.

The method is simple. Take a pure woollen item (this applies to worn woollen blankets too) and put it in the washing machine on a hot wash cycle with about half the detergent you would normally use, do not use fabric softener. If you are worried about shedding fibres, place the item in an old pillow case (see Laundering). It's advisable to remove any buttons or trims before you start, unless they are to form part of your new design. Line long sleeves from cuff to armhole with old nylon tights [pantyhose]. Later, you can open the sleeves out flat and you will have twice the amount of fabric. You should be aware that colours may run at high washing temperatures and shrinkage can be around 30 per cent. Drying in a dryer will help the felting process. Repeated washing and drying will shrink things further, as much as 70 per cent.

Felt fabric doesn't fray and can be made up into virtually anything, from hats and bootees to bags, beads and novelty shapes for appliqué work.

A useful 'scrappy' blanket can be constructed from 8-10 men's thick-knit sweaters (the finer type don't shrink so well) felted in a hot wash and tumble drier before cutting into 18 cm [7 in] squares. Line up the squares in their final pattern and, using satin or close zigzag stitch, machine sew together edge–to-edge, into strips of the desired length. Divide the number of strips by two and join each group vertically to form two equal blanket sides. Finally, pin the two completed halves, wrong sides together, and join round the edges with an overlocking stitch. Straight stitch through both layers along the strip seams to hold the patchwork together, or tie decorative knots of contrasting yarn in the centre of every other square (see p. 90).

KNITTING ABBREVIATIONS AND TERMS

( ) or [ ] Work instructions within parentheses or brackets as many times as directed

* repeat instructions following the asterisk as directed

* * repeat instructions between asterisks, as directed

across to end of row

alt alternate

ball/yarn band the label around a ball of yarn

beg beginning

cast [bind] off secure stitches at finish of work

cast [bind] on assemble stitches before starting work

cm centimetre

cn cable needle

DK double knitting, slightly finer yarn than worsted weight

dec decrease

dpn double pointed needle

eor every other row

FC front cross (to work a cable)

fasten off cutting off and securing yarn tail through final loop

g-st garter stitch

gm gram

inc(s) increase(s)

in inch

k knit

k up 1 lifted increase knitwise

k2tog knit two stitches together

k-wise knitwise

LC left cross (to work a cable)

LH left hand

LN left needle

lp(s) loop(s)

LT left twist (two stitches cross, to work a cable)

M1 make 1 stitch

MB make bobble

MC main colour

m-st moss stitch

multiples number of stitches required to complete a pattern repeat

p purl

p2tog purl two stitches together

patt pattern

prev previous

psso pass slipped stitch over

pu pick up stitch(es)

p up 1 lifted increase purlwise

p-wise purlwise

RC right cross (to work a cable)

rem remaining

rep repeat

rev st st reverse stocking [stockinette] stitch

RH right hand

rib ribbing, vertical columns of knit and purl stitches

RN right needle

rnd round, in circular knitting a row is called a round

row completed series of stitches worked from one needle to the other

RS right side

RT right twist (two stitches cross, as in cable stitch)

selvedges [selvages] the edges formed by the first and last stitches in a row

sk skip or miss

skp(o) same as sl 1, k1, psso

sl st slip stitch

sp space

ssk slip, slip, knit decrease

ssp slip, slip, purl decrease

st(s) stitch(es)

st st stocking [stockinette] stitch

tbl through back loop

tension [gauge] number of stitches and rows to a given measure

tog together

WS wrong side

yb yarn behind

ybk yarn back

yfwd yarn forward

yo yarn over

yon yarn over needle

yrn yarn round needle

CROCHET ABBREVIATIONS AND TERMS

( ) or [ ] Work instructions within parentheses or brackets as many times as directed

* repeat instructions following the asterisk as directed

* * repeat instructions between asterisks, as directed

across to end of row

alt alternate

ball/yarn band the label around a ball of yarn

beg beginning

bet between

bl back loop

bp back post

bpdc back post double crochet

bptr back post treble crochet

ch chain stitch

chs chains

ch-sp chain space

cl cluster

cm centimetre

cont continue

dc double crochet

dc2tog work two double crochet together

dtr2tog work two double trebles together

dec decrease

fasten off cutting off and securing yarn tail through final loop

fl front loop

fp front post

fptr front post treble crochet

foll following

gm gram

htr half treble crochet

in(s) inch(es)

inc increase

LH left hand

lp(s) loop(s)

magic loop yarn loop foundation for working in rounds, producing a neat closed centre

MC main colour

multiples number of stitches required to complete a repeat of a pattern

patt pattern

pc picot

post vertical portion of stitch, see stem

pull up a loop yarn round hook and pull a loop through the stitch below

rem remaining

rep repeat

RH right hand

rnd round, in spirally-worked crochet a row is called a round

row completed series of stitches worked across from one end to the other

RS right side

sk skip or miss

ss slip stitch

sp(s) spaces

st(s) stitch(es)

stem vertical portion of stitch, see post

tbl through back loop

t-ch turning chain

tension [gauge] number of stitches and rows to a given measure

tog together

top of stitch space below front and back loops and above third horizontal thread of stitch

tr treble crochet

ttr triple treble

tr2tog work two trebles together

WS wrong side

yo yarn over

yoh yarn over hook

yrh yarn round hook